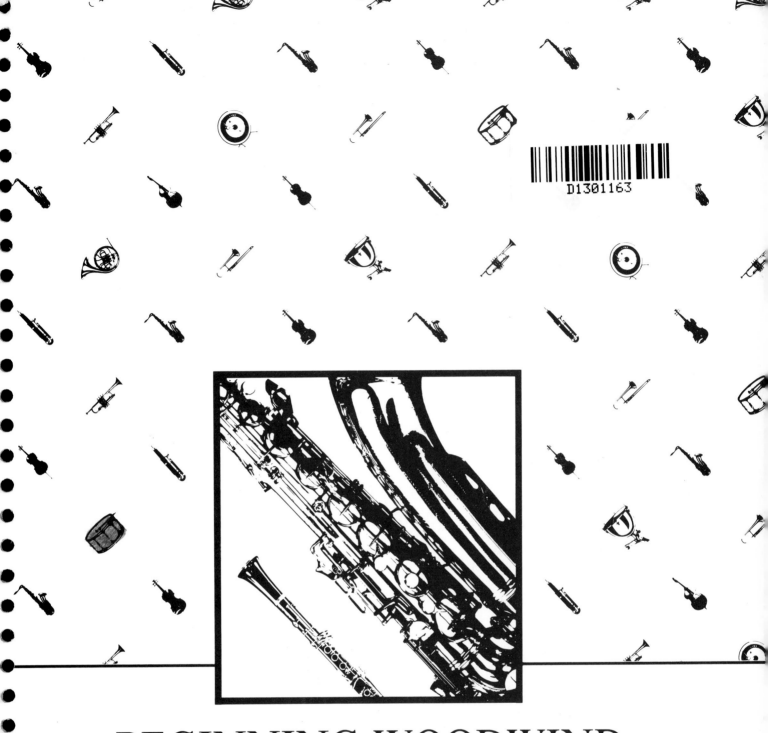

BEGINNING WOODWIND
CLASS METHOD

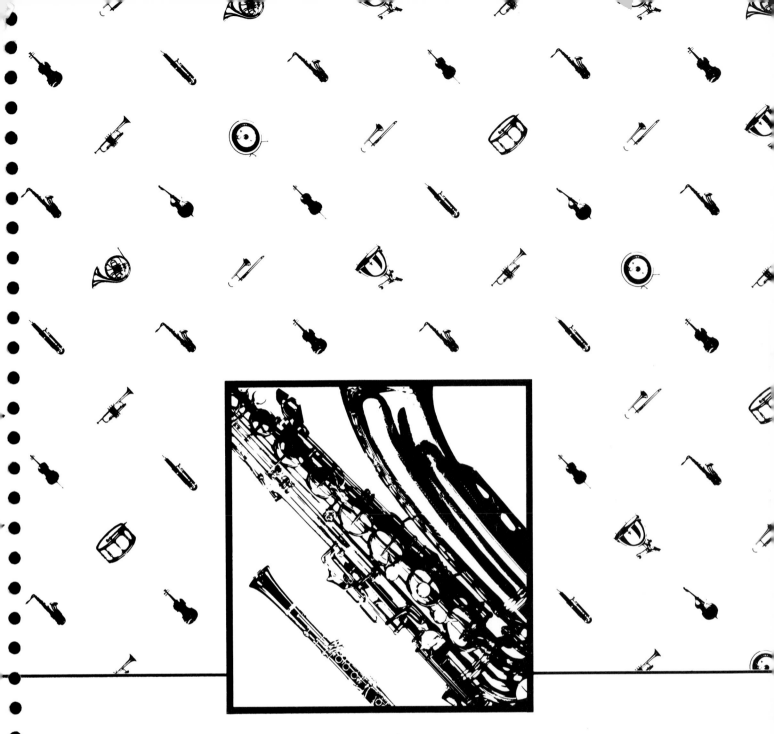

BEGINNING WOODWIND
CLASS METHOD

(WOODWIND ENSEMBLE METHOD)

FREDERICK W. WESTPHAL

CALIFORNIA STATE UNIVERSITY, SACRAMENTO

FOURTH EDITION

wcb

WM. C. BROWN COMPANY PUBLISHERS
DUBUQUE, IOWA

Consulting Editor
Frederick W. Westphal
California State University, Sacramento

Printed in the United States of America

2   03565   01

To Hinda who provided the encouragement
and opportunity which made completion
of this book possible.

Contents

Contents

Illustrations

Preface

This is a beginning woodwind method designed specifically for college/university students. It takes full advantage of previously learned skills in music. There is no provision for instruction in rhythm or note reading which are an essential part of methods designed for public school level students. Musical materials as well are selected with the mature student in mind.

Instructional materials for all woodwind instruments—Flute, Clarinet, Oboe, Bassoon, Alto Saxophone and Tenor Saxophone—are included. This method can be used successfully with any combination of woodwind instruments. Flexible scoring is used in all of the ensemble material so that musical balance can be achieved with a variety of instrumental combinations.

Since the collegiate beginning woodwind class is designed primarily to prepare for future teaching of these instruments this is the focus of the text. Its purpose is to provide an efficient means for acquiring a basic playing facility while at the same time presenting concepts and procedures which will support future teaching of these instruments to students on more advanced proficiency levels.

To accomplish this objective this text goes far beyond the levels commonly found in a beginning instrumental text. Not only are the fundamentals of performance techniques presented and developed but concepts for more advanced performance not commonly a part of a beginning text are introduced and material provided to develop them.

Because of the limitations of time, not all students can be expected to develop a high level of personal performance in all of these aspects, but an understanding of concepts and how these various problems are approached on each instrument will give an excellent foundation to future teaching. These more advanced problems include:

- Essential alternate fingerings with directions on how and when to use them.
- Articulated G-sharp on oboe and saxophone
- Bassoon flick keys

- Half-hole technique for clarinet
- Double and triple tonguing for flute
- Crossing the break techniques
- Trills
- Vibrato
- An extensive fingering chart for each instrument for current and future reference.

Publication of the text in an easy to read score format is designed not only to provide for all the instruments in a single text but to give students an opportunity to observe and learn about instruments other than the one they are studying at the time by relating, comparing and contrasting all of the instruments in the class.

In order to provide for normal individual differences in the rate of progress at this beginning level and to give students an opportunity to progress at their own rate within the class structure three kinds of musical options are provided: (1) Use of two-part and three-part music in which there is a difference in the difficulty of the parts; (2) The use of optional octaves in many examples where more advanced students may increase their facility; and (3) A section of flexible daily studies of basic technique which the student is encouraged to use to the fullest extent. This flexibility will, as well, give woodwind doublers the means to rapidly gain basic competency on one or more additional woodwind instruments.

This text's purpose is to provide the basis for personal competencies on the instruments. The author's companion text *Guide to Teaching Woodwinds* provides extensive additional detailed information on the problems of teaching and playing each instrument so that effective instruction can be given on all levels of achievement.

The author is indebted to many people for their assistance in the preparation of this book. To Len Cramer for photographs not otherwise acknowledged. To the following for posing for photographs: Joanne Mizutani, flute; Gail Coughran, oboe; Alan Wilson, clarinet; Richard Schroder, saxophone; and Armen Phelps, bassoon.

Introduction

This book is designed to provide an opportunity for students to progress at their own rate of accomplishment within the framework of regular class study. Take full advantage of the optional material provided, and assume personal responsibility in adding it to your daily practice.

Read the instructions preceding the various exercises carefully, and make sure you understand them completely before playing. A broader understanding of the entire woodwind group can be achieved through reading and understanding instructions for all the instruments.

PERFORMANCE STYLES AND TECHNIQUES. There is considerable diversity of opinion among authorities on all facets of woodwind technique: embouchure formation, breathing, hand position, tonguing, etc. The very fact that there is such a variety of approaches to the problems is a clear indication that there are several ways in which each of these technical problems can be solved, since the musical result is the same in each instance.

Follow the advice of your instructor. He may want to use a different approach to some of the problems. The directions given in this book represent one of the standard approaches to woodwind playing which is widely used. It may be used with confidence, but it is not the only approach.

PRACTICE. For the most rapid progress on your instrument a weekly practice schedule must be set up and maintained. This should preferably extend over a full seven day period. Much more will be accomplished in practicing thirty minutes per day than in practicing two hours in one day and not touching the instrument for the remainder of the week. After the first few lessons, many students may find it helpful to practice with one or two other members of the class in order to prepare the ensemble material provided. This will add interest and stimulation to the practice period.

The use of a mirror to establish the correct playing position and embouchure is very important. Each student should have a small mirror which he can place on the music stand to make regular checks on embouchure formation.

DAILY STUDIES. After the first few lessons each practice session should begin with appropriate sections of the Daily Studies (exercises 87-93). Regular use of these will facilitate technical development. Each practice session should include some review of previously assigned material. Once an exercise is assigned it should be kept in the practice schedule until mastered. Many students find that new material being practiced for the first time is accomplished easier if the fingering pattern is established silently before playing.

INSTRUMENTS. Instruments used in beginning study must be in good mechanical condition and properly maintained. Careful assembly, disassembly, and handling is necessary. Instruments in poor condition make poor players. A woodwind instrument is a delicate piece of machinery and should be so treated.

REEDS. Even with instruments in the best condition success in playing oboe, clarinet, saxophone, and bassoon is completely dependent upon a good reed. The greatest care and attention must be given to the selection and care of the reed. Seek the advice and assistance of your instructor or a fellow student who is majoring on the instrument. Never handicap yourself by playing on a worn out or damaged reed! For a complete discussion of how to select and adjust reeds see the author's *Guide to Teaching Woodwinds*.

PERFORMANCE OF ROUNDS. A number of rounds are included in this book. Numbers above the staff indicate points at which another voice enters. All rounds should be established as a unison exercise before playing in parts. In performance these rounds may be repeated any number of times, with each part playing through twice as a minimum.

These rounds may be performed by any combination of instruments, and in several different ways:

1. *Parts begin and end one at a time.* This is the traditional manner of performing a round. Each part enters at the appropriate place, plays through at least twice and stops at the end, so that parts reach their conclusion one at a time and in the order in which they started.

2. *Parts begin one at a time and end together.* Each part enters at the appropriate place, plays through at least twice, but continues to play until the signal to end. In this type of performance all parts stop together when any one of the parts has reached the tonic chord tone in the final measure.

3. *Parts begin and end together.* All parts start simultaneously at the points where they would enter under one of the previous types of performance. Play through at least twice stopping when one of the parts reaches the tonic chord tone in the final measure.

Preparation for Playing

In the section which follows study the material for the instrument you are to play. Pay particular attention to the photographs. You should accomplish the following:

1. Learn to identify the parts of the instrument.
2. Practice assembling and disassembling the instrument carefully, replacing parts in their proper places in the case.
3. Establish the proper holding position.
4. Establish the guide position for the hands.
5. Learn to form the proper embouchure as given in the book or directed by your instructor.
6. Accomplish preliminary tone production.
7. Learn how to care for your instrument and reeds.
8. Learn how your instrument is tuned.
9. Study the fingering chart and learn how to read it easily. Identify holes and keys in relation to the fingers used to operate them.

Learning to play a woodwind instrument can be a pleasant and enjoyable experience. It is the hope of the author that this book will make it so.

FLUTE

PARTS OF THE FLUTE

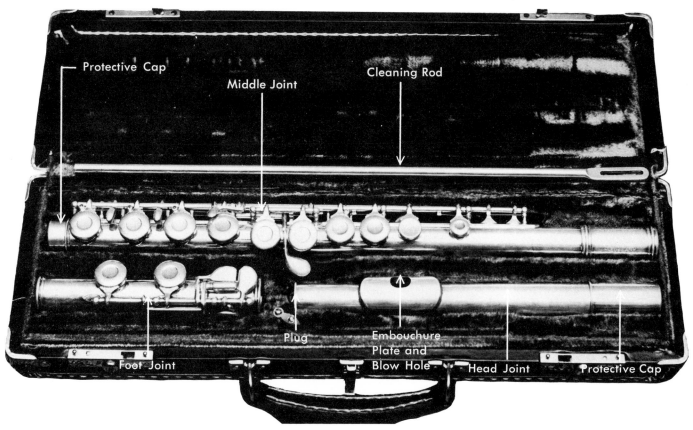

FIGURE 1. Parts of the Flute

ASSEMBLING THE FLUTE

Correct assembly and disassembly of your instrument will help keep it in the best playing condition, and help establish the proper playing position. The following procedure is an efficient one for beginners:

1. Remove the protective cap from the middle joint and hold it by the end away from the mechanism.

2. Take the foot joint by the end below the key mechanism and attach it to the middle joint with a slight winding motion back and forth. Line up the foot joint so that the rod on which the keys pivot is exactly centered with the keys on the top of the middle joint.

3. Remove the protective cap from the head joint and holding the middle joint at the top away from the key mechanism, attach the two with a slight winding motion. Line up the head joint so that the embouchure hole is in a straight line with the keys on the top of the instrument.

FLUTE PLAYING POSITION

1. The flute is held to the right of the body with the instrument angling slightly downward. The head is tilted so that the line of the lips follows the line of the flute. Head erect except for a slight tilt to the right; eyes straight ahead; shoulders turned naturally to the right;

FIGURE 2. Flute Playing Position

elbows free from body; wrists flat and adjusted to the proper finger positions (Figure 2). In a seated position, turn the chair slightly to the right so that the back corner will not interfere with right arm or shoulders.

2. *Left Hand.* The body of the flute rests on the index finger between the knuckle and the first joint. The thumb is curved slightly to contact the B-natural or B-flat lever slightly above the middle joint (Figure 3).

Flute

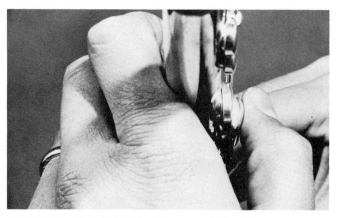

FIGURE 3. Flute Left Index Finger and Thumb

3. To reach the proper holes the index finger has a considerable curve, the other fingers less curve, with the little finger almost straight. The cushions of the fingers contact the keys in the center of the indentations (Figure 4).

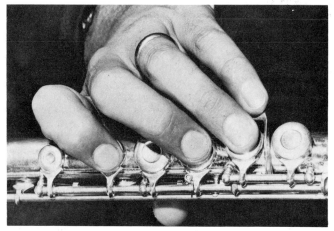

FIGURE 4. Flute Left Hand Position

4. *Right Hand.* The body of the flute is supported on the cushion of the thumb contacting the tube opposite the space between the first and second fingers (Figure 5).

FIGURE 5. Flute Right Thumb Position

5. The little finger helps balance the instrument by pressing the D-sharp key (on all notes except D-natural). Cushions of the remaining fingers contact the center of the indentations of their keys (Figure 6).

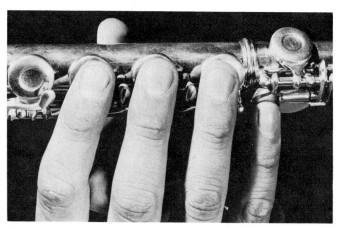

FIGURE 6. Flute Right Hand Position

6. *Guide Position.* The instrument is held securely through support of the right thumb and the index finger of the left hand, assisted by the right little finger and the contact of the lower lip with embouchure hole. With the addition of the left finger touching lightly but not pressing the G-sharp key a guide position (Figure 7) is set up which will maintain the correct playing position and facilitate rapid progress in performance. Check this guide position often, until it becomes automatic.

FIGURE 7. Flute Guide Position

EMBOUCHURE FORMATION

Follow the directions of your instructor, or use the following procedure which is one of the standard flute embouchure formations. Check constantly with a mirror until the formation becomes established.

1. Hold the head joint with the embouchure hole against the lips. Feel with the tongue so that the hole is centered on the lips.

2. Roll the joint forward until the embouchure hole is parallel with the floor, and so that the lower lip covers one-fourth to one-half of the hole.

3. Keeping the lower lip relaxed, pull the corners of the mouth back slightly to firm the upper lip.

4. Allow the center of the upper lip to relax and produce an opening no more than one-sixteenth of an inch high and one-half inch long. The desirable opening is

FIGURE 8. Flute Embouchure

more of a diamond shape than an oval.   It should never be circular.

5. When this is established proceed with preliminary tone production.

PRELIMINARY TONE PRODUCTION

Before producing a tone on the instrument practice with the head joint alone:

1. Hold the head joint with the left hand and stop the open end with the right. Using standard abdominal breath support, blow a gentle concentrated stream of air through the hole in the lips directed toward the opposite edge of the embouchure hole rather than down into it. Move the lower jaw and lips slowly back and forth until a tone which

approximates is produced.

2. Continue to experiment with the speed of air through the lips and the adjustment of the lower jaw and lips until a rather full steady tone can be sustained for at least ten seconds.

3. Open the end of the head joint and repeat the process to produce a pitch which approximates:

4. A slightly greater pressure of the breath, and a change in its direction achieved by pushing the jaws and lips slightly more forward rather than down is necessary to produce this pitch.

5. If these two pitches are produced easily, experiment to produce two notes, using a greater velocity of air and adjusting the lower jaw and lips to produce the higher pitch:

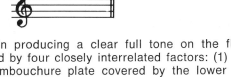

Closed end:

Open end:

Success in producing a clear full tone on the flute is determined by four closely interrelated factors: (1) the amount of embouchure plate covered by the lower lip, (2) the direction of the stream of air, (3) the focusing of a concentrated stream of air determined by the size and shape of the aperture formed by the lips, and (4) the use of standard abdominal breathing and breath support.

CARE OF THE FLUTE

The instrument must be thoroughly cleaned and put in its case after each use. Disassemble in the reverse order of assembly, holding the instrument as instructed to prevent damage to key mechanism. Use a soft lint-free handkerchief or chamois skin in the cleaning rod to dry the inside. Wipe the outside with a soft cloth. Do not use silver polish on the flute, unless specifically directed by your instructor. If dust accumulates beneath the key mechanism it can be removed with a soft watercolor brush. The mechanism should be oiled three or four times a year. A special "key oil" is commercially available. A drop of oil on the end of a needle or toothpick, or with the applicator provided with the oil, should be put at each pivot screw of each key.

Keep the protective caps in place. Keep inside and outside of connecting joints clean so the instrument can be assembled easily. If joints are clean and the instrument is still difficult to assemble, use a small amount of prepared joint grease, or in an emergency a small amount of vaseline. Instruments in good condition do not need this lubrication.

Place the parts in the case carefully with the keys up. Figure 1 gives a typical arrangement of parts in the case. There is only one correct way in which the parts will fit. Do not force the case closed. If it doesn't close easily, check the arrangement of the parts in the case.

Keep the instrument away from all sources of heat and out of direct sunlight.

TUNING AND INTONATION

The flute is a nontransposing instrument, i.e., "A" played on the flute sounds "A" on the piano, the music sounding exactly as written. A-440 is the standard tuning note for the instrument, although bands frequently use B-flat instead, since this is a better tuning note for the brass instruments. For accuracy the tuning note should be sounded by a tuning fork, tuning bar, or electronic

Flute

tuner, or checked with an electronic aid. Tune with the piano if playing with one, or if no other comparison source is available. Even with regular tuning, pitch on a piano fluctuates and is not the best source for a tuning note.

In the very beginning stages of learning to play, tuning and intonation present some difficulties. However as the embouchure develops and technical facility is increased, more and more attention must be given to intonation and tuning. Use of an electronic aid such as the stroboscope is invaluable.

The flute is tuned with the head joint. Pulling the head joint out from the middle joint makes the overall pitch of the instrument flatter, pushing it in makes it sharper. Most flutes are made to sound A-440 with the head joint slightly out from the middle joint.

The plug at the end of the head joint determines the basic intonation of the instrument with itself, and must never be used for tuning. Once set in the proper posi-

tion the plug must never be moved. The proper adjustment of the plug is made with the use of the cleaning rod provided with the instrument. The plug is adjusted so that the line etched on the cleaning rod is exactly in the center of the blowhole when the rod is inserted in the head joint and is against the plug. The intonation may be checked or, in the absence of a cleaning rod, set by adjusting the plug so that the three "D's" are in tune with each other. In teaching careful attention to the adjustment of this plug is necessary since young students pull it out of position by turning the screw cap. Frequently serious intonation problems which students have can be solved by a simple adjustment of the plug.

Once the instrument itself is accurately tuned to the standard pitch, the remainder of the intonation on the instrument is dependent on the player. The intonation is controlled primarily by the embouchure with the assistance of proper breath support. Good intonation is the product of careful and continuous attention.

OBOE

PARTS OF THE OBOE

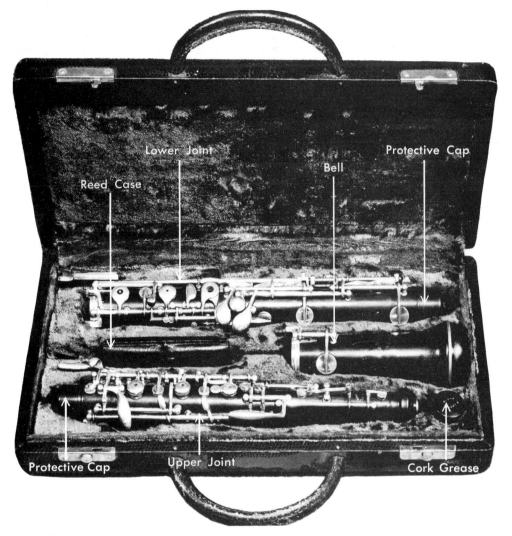

FIGURE 9. Parts of the Oboe

ASSEMBLING THE OBOE

The key mechanism of the oboe is both complicated and delicate, and it is of the utmost importance that assembly and disassembly be done carefully. Before starting the assembly process be sure that all cork joints are well lubricated with prepared cork grease. Do not put pressure on keys or rods when putting the instrument together. The following procedure is an efficient one for beginners:

1. To place the bell on the lower joint, grasp the bell in the right hand with the thumb closing the pad so that the lever which connects with the lower joint is raised. The lower joint is held in the left hand near its lower end and avoiding pressure on keys and rods. Push the two parts together with a slight twisting motion. Line up the two parts of the connecting lever.

2. Putting the upper and lower joints together must be done with extreme care, since there are three (more or less depending on the model of the instrument) connecting levers between the two parts which must be kept in perfect adjustment if the instrument is to play properly.

Grasp the upper joint with the left hand with the fingers depressing the keys to raise the connecting levers and the lower joint in such a way that the keys are *not* depressed. Hold the bottom of the joints toward you and watch the connecting levers while joining the two parts with a slight twisting motion. Line up the connecting levers.

3. Push on the reed firmly, lining up the flat side with the keys on the top of the instrument.

OBOE PLAYING POSITION

1. The oboe is held directly in the center of the front of the body (Figure 10); the instrument at about a 40° angle with the body (Figure 11). Head erect, chin up, eyes straight ahead, with the shoulders up but relaxed. Elbows should hang naturally away from the sides of the body.

2. The right thumb contacts the thumb rest on the flesh to the side of and at the base of the nail, with the ball of the thumb against the body of the instrument (Figure 12).

5

FIGURE 10. Oboe Playing Position Front View

FIGURE 11. Oboe Playing Position Side View

FIGURE 12. Oboe Thumb Positions

3. The right little finger touches the C key lightly, and the remaining fingers fall naturally into position no more than an inch directly above the three tone holes. Let the tips of the fingers overlap the plates slightly so that the ball of the finger is in the center of the plate.

4. The left thumb assists in balancing the instrument and controls the first octave key. It is placed at an angle across the instrument so that the fleshy part of the ball is against the wood of the instrument, with the side touching but not pressing the octave key (Figure 12). The octave key is controlled by vertical movements of the first joint of the thumb in most instances. In some instances, however, the best finger coordination can be achieved by removing the thumb from the instrument just before it is to be used.

5. The left little finger touches lightly the B key and the remaining fingers fall naturally into position not more than an inch directly above the three tone holes.

6. *Guide Position.* With the hands and fingers in this position a *guide position* (Figure 13) is established which should be consistently maintained. Observe that the fingers approach the instrument from a slight upper angle, and the wrists are flat.

In fingering the instrument the entire finger moves from the knuckle and closes the tone holes with a snap or click, pressing just hard enough to close the holes. Avoid too much pressure against the plates with the fingers.

EMBOUCHURE FORMATION

Follow the directions of your instructor, or use the following which is one of the standard formations for oboe. Check regularly with a mirror until the formation becomes established.

FIGURE 13. Oboe Guide Position

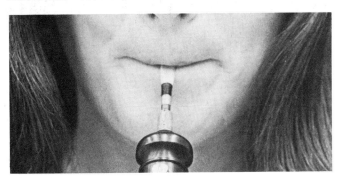

FIGURE 14. Oboe Embouchure

1. With lips relaxed, drop the lower jaw so that the teeth are about a half-inch apart. Place the tip of the reed in the center of the lower lip.

2. Roll the lower lip over the teeth until the tip of the reed is sticking just past the lip. Keeping the lower jaw down, bring the upper lip barely over the teeth.

3. Bring the lips together, pushing the corners of the mouth slightly toward the reed so that the reed is supported with slight pressure from all directions.

4. Keep the lower jaw open so that there is minimum pressure against the reed with the lower teeth.

5. When this is established, proceed with preliminary tone production.

PRELIMINARY TONE PRODUCTION

Before producing a tone on the instrument practice with the reed alone.

1. The reed must be properly moistened each time it is used in order to reach its normal playing shape and so that the correct response can be achieved. Place the reed tip down in about a half-inch of water for five minutes, more or less depending on the cane. Only the blade of the reed should be in the water. Never let the water reach the fishskin covering.

2. Form the embouchure, checking continually in a mirror to see that it is correct.

3. Using a little more reed in the mouth than will be used in playing on the instrument, produce a sound, using standard abdominal breath support.

4. Continue blowing, checking embouchure formation, until the characteristic "double crow" can be produced and sustained for five to ten seconds.

5. When this is accomplished put the reed on the instrument, adjust the amount of reed in the mouth to the proper playing position and practice exercise 1.

The selection and adjustment of a reed for a beginner is highly critical. A good reed for a beginner blows quite easily, and will produce a reedy quality on the instrument which will improve as the embouchure strengthens.

CARE OF THE OBOE

The instrument must be thoroughly dried and put in its case after each use. Wooden instruments crack if moisture is left in them. Disassemble with the utmost care in the reverse order of assembly.

Dry the inside of each piece thoroughly with swabs. At least three types of swabs are available for the oboe: wool swabs, cloth or chamois swabs, and feathers. The only criteria for swab selection is that the entire inside of the instrument be thoroughly dried. Be sure you have swabs which will dry the entire inside of the instrument, including the top joint. Swab each part several times if necessary.

Put the protective caps in place and put the parts in the case carefully with the keys up. Figure 9 gives a typical arrangement of parts in the case. There is only one correct way in which the parts will fit. Do not force the case closed. If it doesn't close easily, check the arrangement of the parts in the case.

Keep the instrument away from all sources of heat and out of direct sunlight.

CARE OF THE OBOE REED

The reed should be blown free of moisture and kept in a special case made for this purpose in order to prevent damage and to keep it from drying out too rapidly. If plastic tubes are used for reed storage, drill small holes in both ends of the tube to provide for air circulation, otherwise the reed will not dry properly. Reeds left loose in the case are soon damaged beyond use. A reed case is a wise investment.

Clean the inside of the reed every week or ten days with a wet pipe cleaner when the reed is well soaked. Insert the wet pipe cleaner through the tube from the cork and force it gently through the tip of the reed. Then pull it through the reed slowly moving it from side to side so that all inside surfaces are cleaned. Repeat the process two or three times.

Keep the fingers off the tip of the reed!

TUNING AND INTONATION

The oboe is a nontransposing instrument, i.e., "A" played on the oboe sounds "A" on the piano, the music sounding exactly as written. A-440 is the standard tuning note for this instrument, although bands frequently use B-flat instead, since this is a better tuning note for the brass instruments. For accuracy the tuning note should be sounded by a tuning fork, tuning bar, or electronic tuner, or checked with an electronic aid. Tune with the piano if playing with one, or if no other comparison source is available. Even with regular tuning, pitch on a piano fluctuates and is not the best source for a tuning note.

In the very beginning stages of learning to play, tuning and intonation present some difficulties. However as the embouchure develops and technical facility is increased, more and more attention must be given to intonation and tuning. An electronic aid such as a stroboscope is invaluable.

On the oboe it is not the instrument itself which is tuned, but the reed. Correct tuning is part of the process of making an oboe reed, and every player who makes his own has an A-440 tuning fork for this purpose. Correct pitch is determined by the length of the reed and by the way in which the lay is cut.

If the reed being used is sharp or flat it can frequently be adjusted to the correct pitch. Seek the assistance of your instructor or a fellow student who is majoring on the oboe. However, reeds made by a professional are carefully tuned and should require little or no adjustment.

Slight adjustments in pitch can be made by adjusting the distance the reed is inserted into the end of the instrument. Pulling the reed out will flatten the overall pitch, pushing it in will sharpen the overall pitch. However, this device must be used with discretion since it also affects the intonation of the instrument with itself as well as ease of playing and tone quality.

If the reed itself is good, once it and the instrument are accurately tuned to the standard pitch, the remainder of the intonation on the instrument is dependent on the player. Intonation is controlled primarily by the embouchure with the assistance of breath support. Good intonation is the product of careful and continuous attention.

CLARINET

PARTS OF THE CLARINET

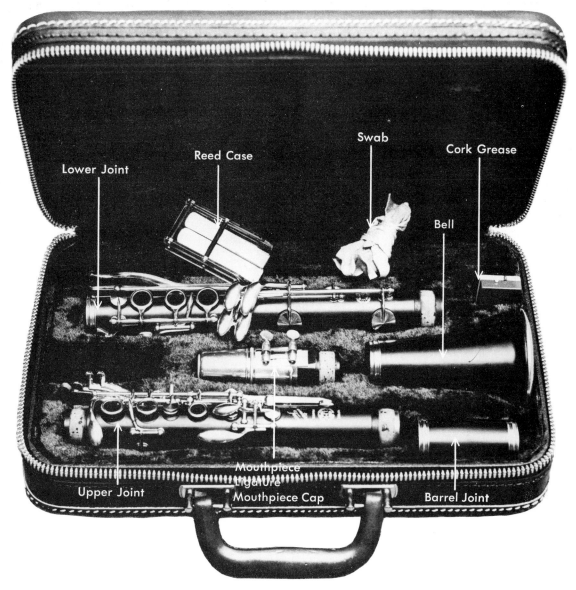

FIGURE 15. Parts of the Clarinet

ASSEMBLING THE CLARINET

Proper assembly and disassembly of your instrument will help keep it in the best playing condition. Do not put pressure on any keys when putting the parts together. Keeping all corks lubricated with cork grease will make assembly of the instrument an easy task. The following procedure is an efficient one for beginners:

1. Put the bell on the lower joint using a slight twisting motion.

2. Pressing down the rings on the upper joint to avoid bending the connecting lever, add it to the lower joint with a slight twisting motion. Line up exactly the two portions of the connecting lever.

3. Add the barrel joint.

4. Add the mouthpiece from which the ligature and reed have been removed, lining up the center of the flat side of the mouthpiece with the register key on the bottom of the clarinet.

ADJUSTMENT OF REED AND LIGATURE

To avoid chipping the tip of the reed, it is best to place the ligature loosely around the mouthpiece first and then slip the reed down inside it. The reed is placed exactly in the center of the lay (the flat part of the mouthpiece). Check both the tip and the butt end of the reed to see that they are properly centered. The tip of the reed should be down from the tip of the mouthpiece so that about a sixty-fourth of an inch of mouthpiece can be seen when looking directly at it. After the reed is properly placed locate the ligature so that its edges are over the guide lines etched in the mouthpiece, and tighten the screws slowly so that the reed is not moved out of place. The ligature should be just tight enough to hold the reed firmly. Proper placement of reed and ligature is of the utmost importance for ease of production and control of tone. Practice reed and ligature adjustment to develop accuracy in placement.

CLARINET PLAYING POSITION

1. The clarinet is held directly in the center of the front of the body (Figure 16), with the instrument at about a 40° angle with the body (Figure 17).

2. The weight of the clarinet is on the right thumb under the thumb rest and balanced between this point and the mouth. The thumb must contact the thumb rest on the flesh to the side of the nail (Figure 18).

3. The thumb of the left hand closes the hole under the instrument and manipulates the register key. This thumb is placed at an angle so that the fleshy part of the ball is closing the hole, and the side of the tip just touching, but not pressing the register key (Figure 19). The register key is controlled by vertical movements of the first joint of the thumb.

4. After thumb positions are established the remaining fingers of each hand lie in a natural curve and close the tone holes with the fleshy parts of the fingers away from the tip. The fingers may approach the clarinet at a slight upper angle with the wrists kept flat.

5. *Guide Position.* The use of the little fingers on guide keys help maintain the correct hand positions. The little finger of the right hand guides by touching lightly but not pressing key F, and the little finger of the left hand guides by touching lightly but not pressing key E.

With the thumbs and little fingers in place, and the remaining fingers no more than one-half inch directly above their respective holes, a guide position of the hands is established (Figure 20) which should be maintained constantly except when the little fingers are used in closing other keys. Proper establishment of this guide position maintains correct hand position and facilitates rapid progress in performance. Check this guide position often until it becomes automatic.

FIGURE 17. Clarinet Playing Position Side View

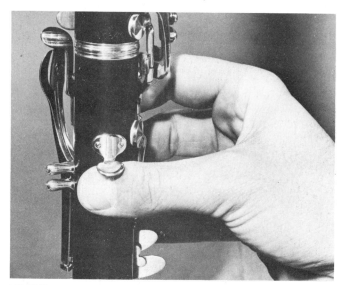

FIGURE 18. Clarinet Right Thumb Position

FIGURE 16. Clarinet Playing Position Front View

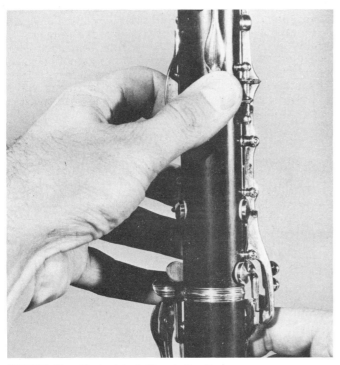

FIGURE 19. Clarinet Left Thumb Position

FIGURE 20. Clarinet Guide Position

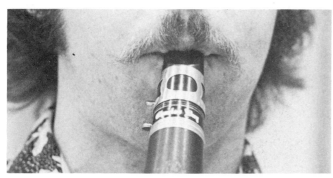

FIGURE 21. Clarinet Embouchure

EMBOUCHURE FORMATION

Follow the directions of your instructor, or use the following procedure which is one of the standard clarinet embouchure formations. Check regularly with a mirror until the embouchure formation becomes established.

1. Keeping the lips lightly together drop the lower jaw so that the teeth are about three-eighths of an inch apart.

2. Shape the lips as if saying the letter "O." The corners of the mouth are slightly compressed and there are wrinkles in the lips.

3. With the mouth dropped and the lips in the "O" position the rim of the lip which divides it from the chin should be directly in front of the top edge of the front teeth. Feel this with a finger and raise or lower the jaw until this relationship is correct.

4. Maintaining this position, insert the mouthpiece of the clarinet into the mouth allowing the reed to push the lower lip over the teeth. If the wrinkles in the lower lip are maintained, the line dividing the lip from the chin is directly over the front edge of the lower teeth. Students with thicker than average lips should adjust so that less lip is over the teeth.

5. Contract the lips and especially the corners of the mouth inward and around the mouthpiece so that there is pressure against the mouthpiece from all directions and no air can escape.

6. The end of the reed must be clear of any contact with the lip for three-eighths to a half inch in order to vibrate freely. Feel this with the tongue.

7. The upper teeth rest, but do not press, on the top of the mouthpiece about a half inch from the end.

8. The lower teeth remain in the open position established in step three above, and must not bite or exert pressure against the lower lip.

9. The chin is held in a firm flat position with a slight downward pressure against the lower lip.

10. Proceed with preliminary tone production described in the following.

PRELIMINARY TONE PRODUCTION

Before producing a tone on the instrument, practice with the mouthpiece alone.

1. Place a carefully selected reed on the mouthpiece in the proper place and adjust the ligature.

2. Form the embouchure, using a mirror to check its formation.

3. Using standard abdominal breath support produce a tone, checking to maintain the proper embouchure formation.

4. Continue practicing until you can produce a steady

natural tone of the highest pitch, approximately for at least ten seconds.

5. When you can do this easily you are ready to proceed with exercise 1.

CARE OF THE CLARINET

The instrument should be thoroughly dried and put in its case after each use. Disassemble in the reverse order of assembly. Dry the inside of each piece thoroughly with a chamois or cloth swab, always putting the swab in the upper end of the piece and drawing it out the lower end. Pull the swab through several times if necessary to completely dry the inside. If dust accumulates beneath the key mechanism it can be removed with a soft watercolor brush. The mechanism should be oiled three or four times a year. A special "key oil" is commercially available. A drop of oil on the end of a needle or toothpick, or with the applicator provided with the oil, should be put at each pivot screw of each key.

Place the parts in the case carefully with keys up. Most instruments will fit in the case only one way. Figure 15 shows a typical arrangement of parts in the case. Do not force the case closed. If it will not close easily check the placement of parts. Forcing the case closed will bend a key so that the instrument will not play properly.

Keep all cork joints well lubricated with prepared cork grease.

Keep instruments away from all sources of heat and out of direct sunlight.

CARE OF THE CLARINET REED

Remove the reed and dry the mouthpiece and reed. Reeds are preferably kept in a reed holder or case especially made for this purpose, although some clarinetists leave the reed on the mouthpiece. Reeds left loose in the case are soon damaged beyond use. Keep the mouthpiece cap in place on the mouthpiece when the instrument is not in use.

TUNING AND INTONATION

The clarinet is a transposing instrument. To sound the standard pitch of A-440 the clarinet plays third-line B.

Bands frequently use B-flat for a tuning note, with the clarinets playing third-space C.

Clarinets are tuned with the barrel joint—never the mouthpiece. All standard brand clarinets are constructed to play slightly sharper than A-440 when the tuning barrel is entirely in. Therefore to tune to A-440 the tuning barrel would normally have to be pulled out approximately a sixteenth of an inch. If the instrument is still sharp, the barrel will have to be pulled further. Pulling the barrel joint out more than a quarter of an inch will frequently make the instrument badly out of tune with itself, as the pitch of some notes is effected more than others. The pitch of the throat tones such as second-line G is flattened more than that of third-line B, for example. If a clarinet student is consistently playing quite sharp or flat so that satisfactory tuning cannot be accomplished with the barrel joint, the cause is in the embouchure, mouthpiece, and/or reed, singly or in combination rather than in the instrument itself.

For accuracy, the tuning note should be sounded by a tuning fork, tuning bar, or electronic tuner, or checked with an electronic aid. Tune with the piano if playing with one, or if no other comparison source is available. Even with regular tuning, pitch on a piano fluctuates and is not the best source for a tuning note.

At the very beginning stages of learning to play, tuning and intonation present some difficulties. However as the embouchure develops and technical facility is increased, more and more attention must be given to intonation and tuning. An electronic aid such as the stroboscope is invaluable.

Good intonation on a clarinet, assuming that the instrument itself is constructed to play in tune, is determined by: (1) a mouthpiece which fits the instrument and whose tone chamber is properly designed, (2) a correctly formed and developed embouchure, and (3) a well adjusted reed which fits both embouchure and mouthpiece. Assuming that all these are right, the intonation on clarinet is controlled primarily by the embouchure with the assistance of proper breath support. Good intonation is the product of careful and continuous attention.

SAXOPHONE

PARTS OF THE SAXOPHONE

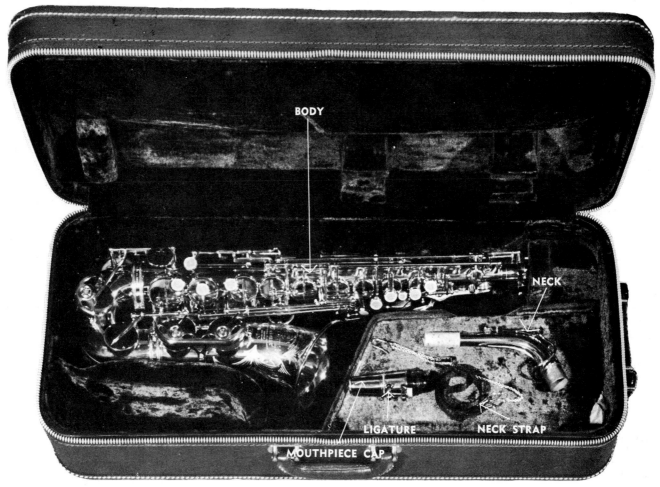

FIGURE 22. Parts of the Saxophone

ASSEMBLING THE SAXOPHONE

The mechanism of the saxophone is rugged, but the long rods, connecting levers, and side keys may be bent out of line if the instrument is not handled carefully. Do not put pressure on keys or rods when putting the instrument together. Before starting the process be sure the cork on the neck of the instrument is well lubricated with prepared cork grease. The following procedure is an efficient one for beginners:

1. Take the neck strap out of the case and put it into position around the neck. Examine the device which adjusts its length, and become familiar with its adjustment.

2. Grasp the instrument by the bell away from the keys. Holding it by the bell, hook the neck strap onto the body. Remove the end plug which protects the connecting lever for the octave key.

3. Check the tension screw(s) which holds the neck in place on the instrument to see that it is loose. Check the sleeve which fits into the body, and the end of the body itself to see that they are clean. If the neck fits into the body of the instrument with difficulty, it may be lubricated with cork grease or vaseline. Hold the neck in the palm of the right hand so the octave key is held down firmly.

Holding the body of the instrument with the left hand, push the neck on. Avoid turning the neck in such a way that the connecting lever will be bent. Line up the brace on the bottom of the neck so that it is centered on the connecting lever on the body of the instrument. Tighten the tension screw to hold the neck firmly in place.

4. Hold the mouthpiece (with the ligature and reed removed) in the palm of the right hand, with the left hand on the neck, palm holding down the octave key. The weight of the instrument is on the neck strap. Push on the mouthpiece so that at least half of the cork is covered, the exact distance is determined by the tuning process. If the instrument has a tuning screw on the neck in addition to a cork, the mouthpiece must be pushed on to cover the entire cork.

ADJUSTMENT OF REED AND LIGATURE

To avoid chipping the tip of the reed it is best to place the ligature loosely around the mouthpiece first, then slip the reed down inside it. The reed is placed exactly in the center of the lay (the flat part of the mouthpiece). Check both the tip and the butt end of the reed to see that they are properly centered. The tip of the reed should be down from the tip of the mouthpiece so that about a sixty-fourth of an inch of the mouthpiece can be seen when looking directly at it. After the reed is properly placed locate the ligature so that its edges are over the guidelines etched in the mouthpiece, and tighten the screws slowly so that the reed is not moved out of place. The ligature should be just tight enough to hold the reed firmly. Proper placement of reed and ligature is of the utmost importance for ease of tone production and control. Practice reed and ligature adjustment to develop accuracy in placement.

SAXOPHONE PLAYING POSITION

1. The saxophone is held to the right of the body with the instrument resting against the side of the leg (Figure 23). The instrument is slightly out of the vertical position with the bottom further back. The right arm is relaxed with the elbow pushed back very slightly to put the right hand into the best playing position (Figure 24). The weight of the instrument is on the neck strap, and is balanced by the right and left thumbs and the mouthpiece in the mouth. Adjust the length of the neck strap so that the end of the mouthpiece touches the center of the lower lip.

FIGURE 24. Saxophone Playing Position Side View

2. The right thumb contacts the thumb rest on the flesh to the side of and at the base of the nail, with the ball of the thumb against the body of the instrument (Figure 25).

3. The left thumb has the function of operating the octave key. It is placed at a diagonal angle across the instrument so that the fleshy part of the ball is on the plate provided for it, and the tip of the finger is touching but

FIGURE 23. Saxophone Playing Position Front View

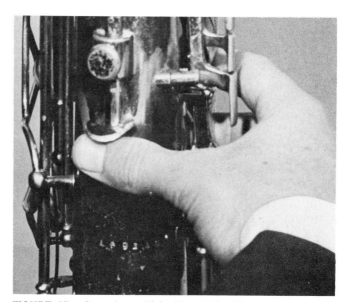

FIGURE 25. Saxophone Right Thumb Position

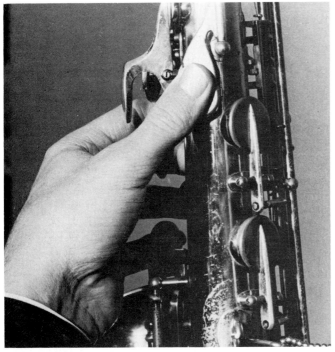

FIGURE 26. Saxophone Left Thumb Position

FIGURE 27. Saxophone Guide Position

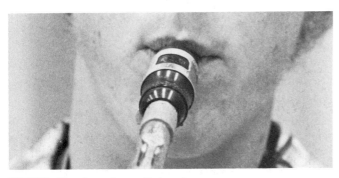

FIGURE 28. Saxophone Embouchure

not pressing the octave key (Figure 26). The octave key is controlled by vertical movements of the first joint of the thumb.

4. *Guide Position.* The left little finger touches lightly the G-sharp key, the right little finger the C key, and the remaining fingers fall into a natural curve without tension to contact the pearl buttons of their tone holes. With all the fingers in position a guide position is established which should be maintained constantly (Figure 27). Check this guide position often until it becomes automatic.

EMBOUCHURE FORMATION

Follow the directions of your instructor or use the following procedure which is one of the standard saxophone embouchure formations. Check regularly with a mirror until the formation is established.

1. Keeping the lips lightly together, drop the lower jaw so that the teeth are about three-eighths of an inch apart.

2. Shape the lips as if saying the letter "O" with the corners of the mouth slightly compressed and there are slight wrinkles in the lips.

3. With the teeth open and the lips in the "O" position the rim of the lower lip which divides it from the chin should be directly in front of the top edge of the front teeth. Feel this with a finger and raise or lower the jaw until this relationship is correct.

4. Maintaining this position, insert the mouthpiece of the saxophone into the mouth allowing the reed to push the lower lip over the teeth. If the wrinkles on the lower lip are maintained, the line dividing the lip from the chin is directly over the front edge of the lower teeth. Students with thicker than average lips should adjust so that less lip is over the teeth.

5. Contract the lips and especially the corners of the mouth inward and around the mouthpiece so that no air can escape.

6. In order to vibrate freely, the end of the reed must be clear of any contact with the lip for three-eighths to a half inch on the alto saxophone, more on the tenor. The amount of mouthpiece in the mouth is determined by the mouthpiece itself—some require more mouthpiece in the mouth than others.

7. The upper teeth rest, but do not press, on the top of the mouthpiece somewhat forward of the position of the lower teeth.

8. The lower teeth remain in the open position established in step three above, and must not bite or exert pressure against the lower lip.

9. The reed and mouthpiece are supported and controlled by inward pressure toward the center of the mouthpiece by the upper and lower lips and by the corners of the mouth.

10. Proceed with the preliminary tone production described in the following.

PRELIMINARY TONE PRODUCTION

Before producing a tone on the instrument, practice with the mouthpiece alone.

1. Place a carefully selected reed on the mouthpiece in the proper place and adjust the ligature.

2. Form the embouchure, using a mirror to check its formation.

3. Using standard abdominal breath support produce a tone, checking to maintain the proper embouchure formation.

4. Continue practicing until you can produce a steady natural tone of the highest pitch for at least ten seconds.

5. When you can do this easily you are ready to proceed with exercise 1.

CARE OF THE SAXOPHONE

The instrument should be thoroughly dried and put in its case after each use. Disassemble in the reverse order of assembly. A swab made for the saxophone is used to clean the inside of the body of the instrument, and a special neck cleaner for the inside of the neck. Using a chamois or soft cloth wipe the inside portion of the bell, then the body of the instrument to keep it clear of fingerprints. If dust accumulates beneath the key mechanism it can be removed with a soft watercolor brush. The mechanism should be oiled three or four times a year. A special "key oil" is commercially available. A drop of oil on the end of a needle or toothpick, or with the applicator provided with the oil, should be put at each pivot screw of each key.

Remove the reed and dry the mouthpiece and reed with a chamois or soft cloth. Reeds are preferably kept in a reed holder or case especially made for this purpose. Reeds left loose in the case are soon damaged beyond use.

Place the parts of the instruments in the case, being sure to replace the plug which fits into the small end of the body. The mouthpiece, ligature, reed case, neck, and neck strap are placed in a small compartment in the case to protect them. Do not force the case closed.

Keep the neck cork well lubricated with prepared cork grease, and the sleeve and its connecting part of the body clean and well lubricated.

Keep all instruments away from all sources of heat and out of direct sunlight.

CARE OF THE SAXOPHONE REED

Remove the reed and dry the mouthpiece and reed. It is best to keep the reed in a reed case for protection and so that it will dry flat. If the reed is stored on the mouthpiece the ligature should not be tight. Reeds left loose in the case are soon damaged beyond use. Keep the mouthpiece cap and ligature in place on the mouthpiece when the instrument is not in use.

TUNING AND INTONATION

Saxophones are transposing instruments. To sound the standard pitch of A-440 the alto saxophone plays F-sharp and the tenor saxophone B-natural. If a B-flat is sounded as a tuning note as it frequently is in bands, the alto saxophone plays G-natural and the tenor saxophone C-natural. The saxophone is tuned with the mouthpiece. If the instrument is flat when tuning, push the mouthpiece further on the cork, if the instrument is sharp when tuning, pull the mouthpiece out so less cork is covered. In general saxophones are made to sound A-440 when approximately half the cork is covered by the mouthpiece. Some saxophones have an adjustable tuning screw on the neck of the instrument in place of a long cork. On these instruments the mouthpiece is placed over the entire cork, and the tuning is done with the screw.

Intonation on a saxophone is determined by several things: (1) the construction of the instrument itself; (2) a mouthpiece which fits the instrument and whose tone chamber is properly designed; (3) a correctly formed and developed embouchure; and (4) a well adjusted reed which fits both embouchure and mouthpiece. Virtually all standard brand instruments are acoustically well in tune, and can be played in tune if other things are correct. Generally speaking a reed which is too hard tends to make the instrument sharp, while a reed which is too soft tends to make the instrument flat. The embouchure is the primary controlling factor in intonation. The amount of mouthpiece in the mouth is critical, too little will make the higher notes flat, too much mouthpiece in the mouth tends to make the general pitch of the instrument flat, as well as making it virtually impossible to control the pitch of individual notes. Biting with the lower teeth causes numerous complications. The angle at which the saxophone is held determines the way in which the embouchure can control it. A standard brand mouthpiece should be suspected of causing intonation problems only after embouchure and reed have been determined to be in good shape.

PARTS OF THE BASSOON

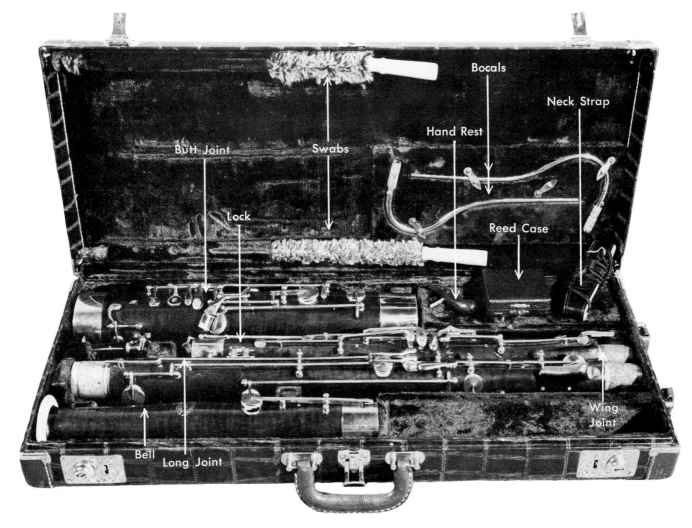

FIGURE 29. Parts of the Bassoon

ASSEMBLING THE INSTRUMENT

The key mechanism of the bassoon is complicated, and the long rods on which some of the keys operate make it of the utmost importance that assembly and disassembly be done carefully. Do not put pressure on keys or rods when putting the instrument together. Before starting the process be sure that all cork joints are well lubricated with prepared cork grease. The following procedure is an efficient one for beginners:

1. Take the neck strap out of the case and put it into position around the neck. Examine the device which adjusts its length, and become familiar with its adjustment.

2. Put the wing joint into the small opening in the butt joint, grasping the wing joint in the left hand with the thumb in the curved portion beneath the cluster of keys and grasp the middle of the butt joint with the right hand. Push the two together with a slight twisting motion, lining up the curved portion of the wing joint with the other hole in the butt. Lay these assembled parts in the case.

3. Grasp the bell joint with the right hand pressing the key with the thumb and put it on the long joint lining up the connecting lever which operates the key.

4. The two assembled sections are then put together, holding the boot and wing joint in the right hand and the bell and long joint in the left. The long joint can be pushed into place with a slight twist.

5. Make final adjustments of the long and wing joints so that they lock together.

6. Insert hand rest for right hand and tighten screw to hold it in place.

7. Grasp the bocal near the cork and put it firmly in place. If the instrument has a whisper key adjust the bocal so that the pad of this key covers the small hole in the bocal.

8. Put the reed firmly in place.

BASSOON PLAYING POSITION

1. The weight of the bassoon is supported by a neck strap or a seat strap, with the lower part of the instrument against the right side of the player and balanced with the left hand. Adjust the height of the instrument with the strap so that when the head is erect the reed will touch the lower jaw just below the lips. The reed can be correctly taken into the mouth from this position.

FIGURE 30. Bassoon Playing Position Side View

FIGURE 31. Bassoon Playing Position Front View

2. The bell of the instrument is inclined toward the player's left so that the music can be seen over the bocal (Figure 31). Head is slightly inclined with the chin up and eyes straight ahead. Shoulders are up but relaxed. The elbows should hang naturally away from the sides of the body, with the right elbow raised slightly to maintain a straight wrist.

3. The left hand balances the bassoon, with the flesh below the knuckles resting against the wing joint (Figure 32). The fingers cover the three holes. The thumb has several keys to close, and must move from joints as well as the base to contact the keys. It is most frequently on the whisper key (Key W).

4. The right hand is best supported with a hand rest attached to the instrument. This hand rest fits in the crotch between the thumb and first finger, leaving the fingers free to cover holes, and the thumb free to close its keys (Figure 33). The use of a hand rest is especially important for beginners.

Keep the fingers slightly curved, using the fleshy part of the fingers away from the tips on the holes, rings, and keys. Keep the fingers one-fourth to one-half inch directly over the proper holes or keys (Figure 34).

5. *Guide Position.* Proper establishment of a guide position (Figure 34) maintains correct hand and finger position and facilitates rapid progress in performance.

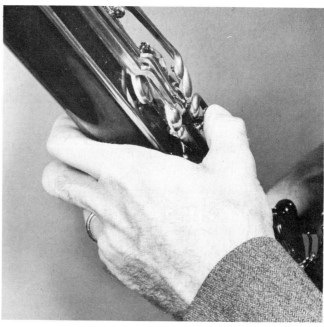

FIGURE 32. Bassoon Left Hand Support

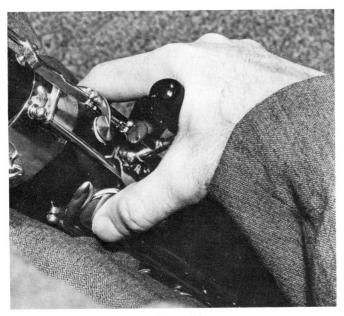

FIGURE 33. Bassoon Right Hand Support

FIGURE 34. Bassoon Guide Position

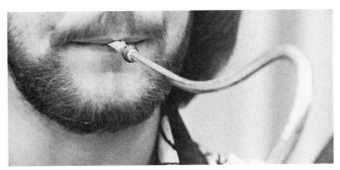

FIGURE 35. Bassoon Embouchure

With the left hand against the tenor joint, the right hand in the hand rest and the fingers directly over the proper holes, the left little finger touches lightly the D-sharp key and the left thumb touches lightly the whisper key—Key W (Figure 32). The right little finger touches lightly the F key, and the right thumb the E key (Figure 33). Thumbs and all fingers maintain this position except when they are used in closing other keys. Check this guide position often until it becomes automatic.

EMBOUCHURE FORMATION

Follow the directions of your instructor, or use the following procedure which is one of the standard bassoon embouchure formations. Check regularly with a mirror until the embouchure formation becomes well established.

1. Keeping the lips relaxed, drop the lower jaw so that the teeth are about a half inch apart.

2. Pull the lower jaw back to increase the natural overbite. The jaw is kept back while playing.

3. Push the corners of the mouth toward the center as in whistling, forming wrinkles in the lips.

4. Maintaining the contracted position of the lips, roll them over the teeth so that virtually all of the lip is over the teeth. The exact amount of lip over the teeth varies from student to student depending on whether the lips are average, thin, or thick. Pull the chin muscles down. Avoid bunching under the reed.

5. Put the reed between the lips. The reed should be in the mouth far enough that the upper lip is almost touching the first wire. Contract the lips around the reed like a drawstring.

6. Continue with the following directions for preliminary tone production, which will establish the exact amount of reed in the mouth.

PRELIMINARY TONE PRODUCTION

1. Before producing a tone on the instrument, practice with the reed alone. The bassoon reed must be soaked each time before playing by placing it tip down in water for three to five minutes. The water should come only to the first wire, since immersing the entire reed may expand the tube and the binding will come loose. Some bindings have a waterproof coating in which case the entire reed may be soaked in water. Check with your instructor.

2. The setting of the embouchure is aimed at finding the exact formation and amount of reed in the mouth which produces the characteristic "double crow" on the reed alone. The well adjusted bassoon reed when blown alone produces a buzz commonly called a "crow" of two distinct pitches—one high and one low pitched. Some good reeds produce more than two pitches but the high and low ones will predominate in the sound.

3. Use a reed which has been prepared for playing and form the embouchure. Starting with just the tip of the reed between the lips produce a sound using standard abdominal breath support. The sound will be a thin, reedy buzz.

4. Keeping the sound continuous gradually increase the amount of reed in the mouth until the upper lip touches the wire on the reed. Considerable differences

in sound will be readily apparent as the amount of reed in the mouth increases. Move it back and forth to note the immediate differences.

5. At some point as the amount of reed in the mouth is changed, the characteristic "double crow" of the bassoon reed will be heard with maximum resonance. This is the critical point on the cut of the reed, normally more than half way between the tip and first wire, and determines the exact amount of reed to be put into the mouth. This point should be approximately centered between the support provided by the upper and lower lips over the teeth.

6. Remember to use a good firm abdominal support of wind pressure while blowing into the instrument. Keep the lower jaw pulled back to increase the natural overbite. Under normal circumstances with a well adjusted reed, the upper lip will almost touch the first wire on the reed in the optimum position.

7. Continue practicing on the reed until the crow is easily produced and you can sustain it for five to ten seconds. When you can do this you are ready to proceed with the entire instrument and exercise 1.

CARE OF THE BASSOON

The instrument must be thoroughly cleaned and put in its case after each use. Disassemble with the utmost care in the reverse order of assembly. Dry the inside of each piece thoroughly with the special swabs provided. Shake and blow the moisture out of the bocal. Keep the joints well lubricated with prepared cork grease. Wipe off the keys and wood with a chamois or soft cloth. Because of the way in which the holes are bored in the instrument, some of them tend to collect moisture. This can be blown out or swabbed out with a folded pipe cleaner. If moisture has collected under a pad, dry the pad with blotting paper or cigarette paper. The bocal may be cleaned by running warm water through it occasionally, and the small hole in it which is closed by the whisper key cleared with a straw.

Place the parts in the case carefully with the proper keys up. Figure 29 shows a typical arrangement of parts in the case. There is only one correct way in which the parts fit. Do not force the case closed. If it doesn't close easily, check the arrangement of parts in the case.

CARE OF THE BASSOON REED

1. Always soak the reed as directed before playing or adjusting.

2. Blow the reed free of moisture when finished playing and keep it in a reed case so that it will dry out slowly and completely to retain its proper form. If a plastic tube is used for reed storage, be sure that there are holes in each end for proper air circulation, otherwise the reed will not dry properly.

3. Clean the inside of the reed every week or ten days with a wet pipe cleaner when the reed is well soaked. Insert the pipe cleaner from the round end and force it gently through the tip of the reed. Then pull it through the reed slowly moving it from side to side so that all inside surfaces are cleaned. Repeat the process two or three times.

4. Keep the outside surfaces of the blades clean so that vibration is not restricted. A light polishing with Dutch Rush will clean the surface.

5. Keep fingers off the tip of the reed.

TUNING AND INTONATION

The bassoon is a nontransposing instrument, i.e., A played on the bassoon sounds A on the piano, the music sounding exactly as written. A-440 is the standard tuning note for orchestra, with the bassoon tuning an octave lower by playing A top line of the bass clef which sounds A-220. Learning to hear a perfect octave requires some practice, but facility is easily acquired. Bands frequently use B-flat as the standard tuning note, since this is a better tuning note for the brass instruments. For accuracy the tuning note should be sounded by a tuning fork, tuning bar, or electronic tuner, or checked with an electronic aid. Tune with the piano if playing with one, or if no other comparison source is available. Even with regular tuning, pitch on a piano fluctuates and is not the best source for a tuning note.

In the very beginning stages of learning to play, tuning and intonation present some difficulties. However as the embouchure develops and technical facility is increased, more and more attention must be given to intonation and tuning. An electronic aid such as a stroboscope is invaluable.

On the bassoon, it is not the instrument itself which is tuned, but the reed. Correct tuning is part of the process of making a bassoon reed, and every player who makes his own has an A-440 or A-220 tuning fork for this purpose. Correct pitch is determined by the length of the reed and by the way in which the lay is cut.

If the reed being used is sharp or flat it can frequently be adjusted to the correct pitch. Seek the assistance of your instructor or a fellow student who is majoring on the bassoon. The author's *Guide to Teaching Woodwinds* gives detailed instructions on reed adjustment.

Very slight adjustments in pitch can be made by adjusting the distance the bocal is inserted into the end of the instrument. Pulling the bocal out will flatten the overall pitch, pushing it in will sharpen the overall pitch. However this must be done in such a way that the small hole in the bocal can be closed by the pad of the whisper key.

Larger adjustments in pitch on the bassoon are made by changing bocals. Most instruments are supplied with two bocals of different lengths. The longer bocal will be flatter in pitch than the shorter one. Experiment with both bocals to determine the one best suited for your playing.

If the reed itself is good, once it and the instrument are accurately tuned to the standard pitch, the remainder of the intonation on the instrument is dependent on the player. Intonation is controlled primarily by the embouchure with the assistance of breath support. Good intonation is the product of careful and continuous attention.

Beginning Fingering Patterns

1. Left Hand Patterns

Check alignment of the instrument; have reed prepared and in the correct position; review holding position of the instrument with special attention to establishing the guide position; form the correct embouchure.

Play the exercise with a full tone, but avoid playing too loudly. Repeat each section at least four times, or until the pattern is played accurately. Maintain the correct hand position and embouchure formation throughout. Use standard abdominal breath support, and take a breath at the end of any slur. A small mirror on the music stand is an essential aid in checking embouchure formation.

FINGERINGS. Familiarize yourself with the identifications for the holes and keys on your instrument given in the photograph with the fingering chart. Check the fingering chart for the proper fingering for each note if it is not provided with the text material. In each instance the first fingering given for a note is the basic standard one. Do not use another fingering unless directed to do so by your instructor or in the text's introductory material to a specific exercise.

Fingers open and close holes and keys with a rapid movement, sometimes described as a "snap" or "click." Do not move the fingers slowly; do not pound the keys; and avoid pressing too hard with the fingers that are down. Instruments in good condition need only a firm pressure to close the holes. The tendency to press too firmly is especially true on the clarinet and bassoon and soon pulls the fingers out of position.

Exercises 1 and 2 are basic orientation to each individual instrument. As such they cannot be played by a mixed ensemble of instruments.

Below are the fingerings for the notes in the first exercise.

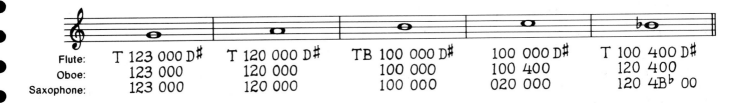

Flute:	T 123 000 D♯	T 120 000 D♯	TB 100 000 D♯	100 000 D♯	T 100 400 D♯
Oboe:	123 000	120 000	100 000	100 400	120 400
Saxophone:	123 000	120 000	100 000	020 000	120 4B♭ 00

| Clarinet: | T 123 000 | T 120 000 | T 100 000 | T 000 000 | T 120 4x00 | 100 000 |

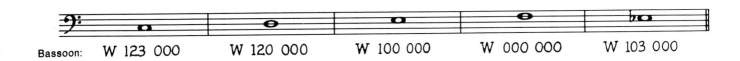

| Bassoon: | W 123 000 | W 120 000 | W 100 000 | W 000 000 | W 103 000 |

2. Right Hand Patterns

Observe the same general directions given for exercise 1. Play with a full tone, adjusting breath support as needed. Some players will find it easier to establish right hand notes in a downward sequence. If you are insecure on the lower note, work downward from the top note until the starting note of the exercise responds easily.

FLUTE: A slightly smaller opening in the lips to produce a more intense stream of air is necessary for these notes. Experiment in moving the head up and down very slightly and/or rolling the flute back and forth slightly to discover the best position for a full tone.

Note that the first finger of the left hand is up for fourth-line D.

Be sure the right little finger is pressing the D♯ key on all other notes.

OBOE: This exercise introduces the use of the half-hole position for the first finger, and the use of octave key A.

The first finger half-hole position is used for these notes:

For the half-hole position the finger is rolled downward—not slid—with a movement of the second joint of the finger so that the vent hole is open and the finger is on the extension plate of this key. The remaining fingers are kept in the guide position.

Octave key A is used on these notes:

Review the position of the left thumb and the operation of octave key A. If the thumb is in the correct position a vertical movement of the first joint of the thumb will open and close the key. Do not slide the thumb.

Two fingerings for:

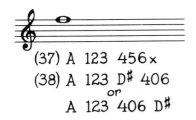

(37) A 123 456x
(38) A 123 D♯ 406
      or
     A 123 406 D♯

These two fingerings are of equal importance. Learn to use both with equal facility. In fingering #38 the D♯ key may be with either the right or left little fingers. It is used only if the instrument you are playing does not have the F resonance key. (If there is a key on the side of the body of the instrument which opens and closes simultaneously with the middle hole of the right hand, the instrument has an F resonance key.)

Fingering #37 is the standard diatonic and chromatic fingering for F. Fingering #38, called the "fork F" is used whenever the sixth finger must be used to cover the hole on the note which precedes or follows the F. Avoid using the sixth finger on the hole and on the F key on consecutive notes. Read ahead to select the proper fingering. Some players mark the proper fingering on the music. Establishing the proper choice of fingerings at this point will pay dividends as your study progresses. Fingering #38 should be used in exercise 2-c-e-h-i.

If the instrument is a good one and the fingers are in the proper position the instrument will respond easily on notes in this exercise.

BASSOON: The bassoon responds easily in this register if the reed is good and the fingers are in the proper position. Keep the reed well in the mouth. Avoid using less reed to play the lower notes, rather, relax the pressure of the lower lip against the reed.

Two fingerings for:

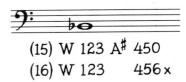

(15) W 123 A♯ 450
(16) W 123   456x

In playing the exercise with the B-flat signature, establish the two fingerings for B-flat. These two fingerings are of equal importance. Learn to use both with equal facility.

Fingering #15 must be used when the sixth finger must cover its tone hole as part of the fingering on the note following or preceding. It must be used in exercise 2-c-e-h-i, in the key of F.

Fingering #16 may be used in diatonic or chromatic passages when the sixth finger is not involved in the fingering of the preceding or following note. It may be used in exercise 2-a-b-d-f-g, in the key of F.

Avoid using the sixth finger on the hole and on the B-flat key on consecutive notes. Read ahead to plan the correct fingering. Establishing the proper choice of fingerings at this point will pay dividends as your study progresses.

Following are the fingerings for notes in Exercise 2.

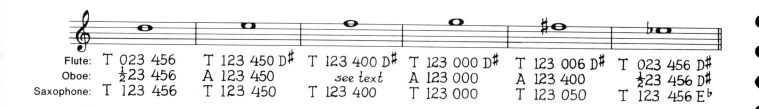

Flute:	T 023 456	T 123 450 D♯	T 123 400 D♯	T 123 000 D♯	T 123 006 D♯	T 023 456 D♯
Oboe:	½23 456	A 123 450	see text	A 123 000	A 123 400	½23 456 D♯
Saxophone:	T 123 456	T 123 450	T 123 400	T 123 000	T 123 050	T 123 456 E♭

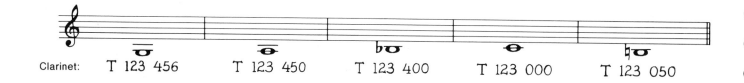

Clarinet:	T 123 456	T 123 450	T 123 400	T 123 000	T 123 050

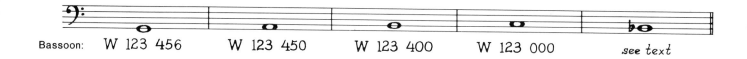

Bassoon:	W 123 456	W 123 450	W 123 400	W 123 000	see text

Class Notes

Right Hand Patterns

FLUTE, OBOE, AND SAXOPHONE

Practice also
using

CLARINET

Practice also
using

BASSOON

Practice also
using

Basic Octave

3-12. Exercises and Repertoire

These exercises and melodies combine the left and right hand finger patterns to make the basic octave for the instrument. Practice them slowly at first to match loudness and quality of the tones, increasing speed as facility increases. Take a breath at the end of any slur.

FLUTE: Practice using both fingerings for B-flat. Remember that the first finger is up on D, and to use the D-sharp key as part of the fingering for all other notes. If breath is being expended too rapidly and you must breathe too often, work toward developing a small opening in the lips, and experiment with the direction and focus of the breath toward the blow hole.

OBOE: Continue to pay particular attention to the use of the half-hole and octave key A, and to develop the proper choice of fingering for F. Note the introduction of fingering #25—103 456 C for third-space C in exercise 4. This fingering matches the tone quality of notes above better than the 100 400 fingering. After both fingerings are established choose the best fingering for a passage on the basis of facility, intonation, and tone quality.

Since the volume of air needed to produce a tone on the oboe is small in comparison with the other woodwind instruments, players frequently have a surplus of air in their lungs. Develop the habit of exhausting the air left in the lungs as part of the process of taking a new breath.

Avoid taking a series of small shallow breaths.

CLARINET: In playing the new note G (000 000) be very particular about keeping the hands in the guide position. The left thumb is held directly over the hole for these notes, it must not touch the instrument.

Use fingering #21—100 000 for F-sharp. Fingering #22—T 000 4xy00 is a special fingering used for chromatics and trills.

BASSOON: Continue to establish the correct selection and use of the two B-flat fingerings. It is very important to establish the proper use of these fingerings at this point. Keep the embouchure formation the same throughout the compass of these exercises. There may be slight changes in pressure of the lower lip against the reed—less for the lower notes, more for the higher ones. Do not change the amount of reed in the mouth.

SAXOPHONE: Check hand positions and operation of the octave key with the left thumb. Alto saxophone should pay particular attention to matching tone quality in the half-step C-sharp to D.

DAILY STUDIES: Appropriate sections of the Daily Studies (exercises 83-91) should be a regular part of your daily practice. From time to time you will be directed to particular sections appropriate to the problem being presented. Take personal responsibility for adding sections of these studies as your facility increases.

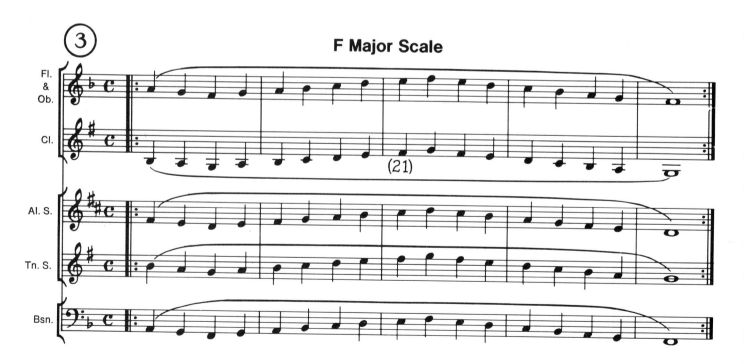

(3) F Major Scale

Fl. & Ob.

Cl.

(21)

Al. S.

Tn. S.

Bsn.

Thirds

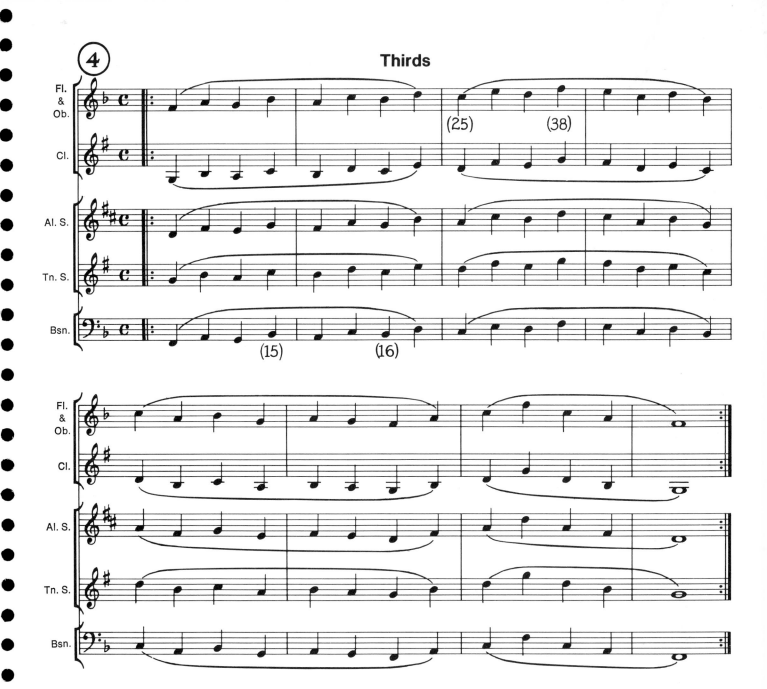

5 Ach Gott und Herr

Chorale

J.S. Bach

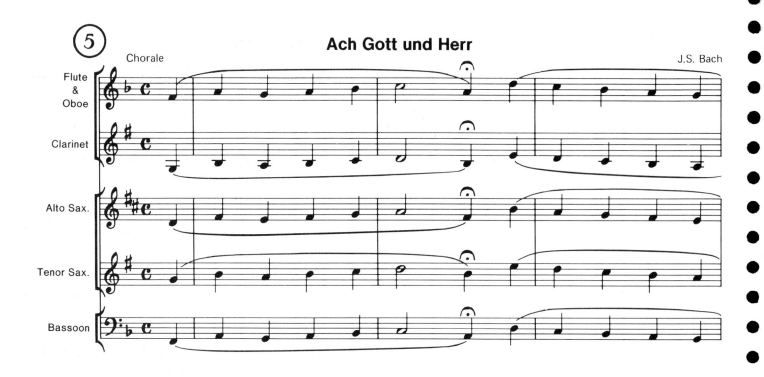

Christus der ist mein Leben

Folk Song

Sum, Sum, Sum

German

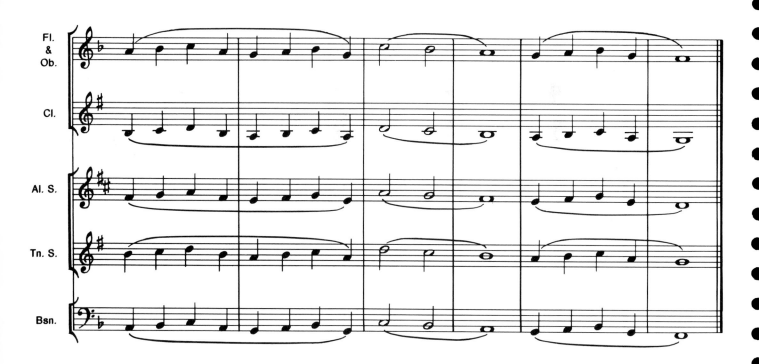

⑧ Four-Part Round   **Do-Re-Mi**   Traditional

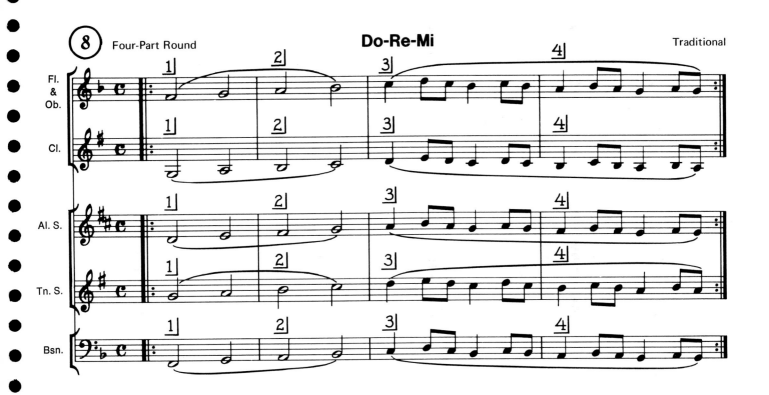

Class Notes

Scale and Third Patterns

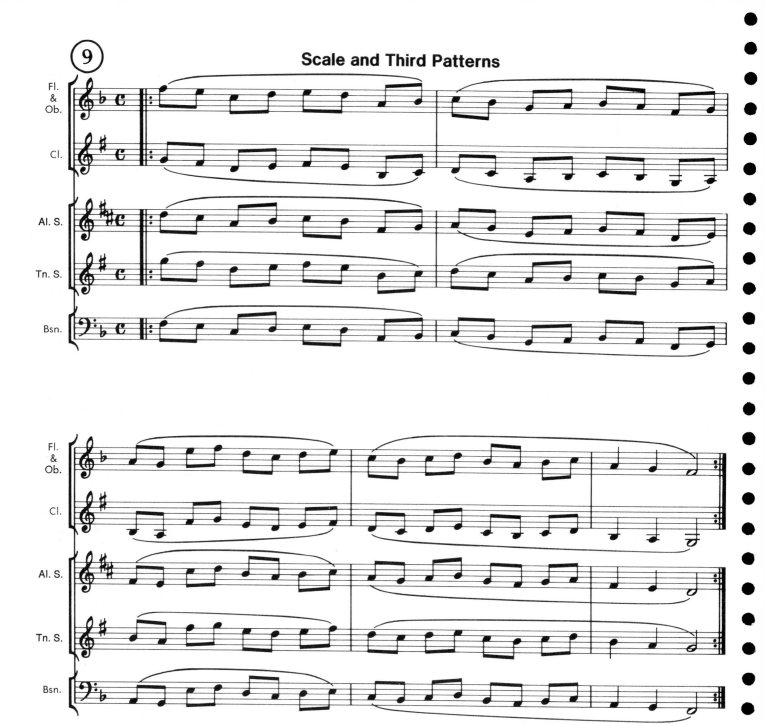

Interval Study

(11) Andante   **Les Moissonneurs**   Couperin

Class Notes

Der Freischutz

Von Weber

Class Notes

Fundamental Articulation

13-18. Fundamental Articulation

During the course of this study the three basic types of articulation or attack will be presented: fundamental articulation, staccato articulation, and legato articulation. Each of these is capable of considerable variation in the hands of a skilled performer, and are essentially the same musically no matter what performance media is being used. For truly artistic performance each must be under perfect control at all dynamic levels, and at all speeds, with the exact sounds being determined by the style of the music being played. Do not let the articulation effect tone quality.

On woodwind instruments these three types of articulations are produced by the tongue interrupting the flow of air through the instrument. The differences in sound are in the amount of space or silence between consecutive notes which determines the length of the notes themselves, and by the hardness of the attack. To start the tone the tongue is put in the proper position, air pressure built up against it, then released by the tongue. No portion of the breathing mechanism is otherwise involved in articulation. The most common fault is that of moving the supporting muscles on each note simultaneously with the tongue action. In any series of notes the breath support must remain constant rather than relaxing when the tongue interrupts its flow. The concept of a constant flow of air interrupted by the tongue is basic to the development of good articulation, and must be assiduously practiced if good articulation is to be achieved.

Fundamental articulation is that most often found, and is used when the notes are not slurred and have no other type of articulation indicated. The notes are well separated, and begun with a firm solid attack.

Exact placement of the tongue for articulation on the various woodwind instruments is the subject of some differences of opinion by various authorities, and there is more than one standard placement for each instrument. Follow the recommendations of your instructor, or use the following directions.

TONGUE PLACEMENT: With the instrument in playing position and the embouchure properly formed, use the following positions of the tongue:

FLUTE: Place the tip of the tongue on the front teeth at the base of the gum.

DOUBLE REED: Touch the lower blade of the reed at the tip with the top of the tongue just back of the tip. Do not plug the tip of the reed. A slight pressure against the reed closes the tip so no air will go through.

SINGLE REED: Feel with the tip of the tongue the junction of the reed and lower lip. The reed and lip form a small "V" shaped pocket. The tongue should be in this pocket with the tip of the tongue curved up and touching the reed lightly three-eighths of an inch from the tip for clarinet, somewhat farther for saxophone. The tongue must not lie flat on the reed. A slight pressure of the tongue against the reed will close the tip against the mouthpiece so no air will escape.

ARTICULATION: Use the following step by step procedure for fundamental articulation:

1. To start the tone with the tongue in place, build up air pressure against it. Be sure no air is escaping.
2. Release the air into the instrument with a tongue action similar to that in pronouncing the syllable "too" or "du."
3. If there is no rest following the note, simply repeat the syllable to articulate the next tone.
4. If a rest follows the note, stop the tone by stopping the flow of air. Do not put the tongue back in place to stop the sound.
5. During the silence of the rest repeat steps one and two to start the next tone.

Repeated Notes

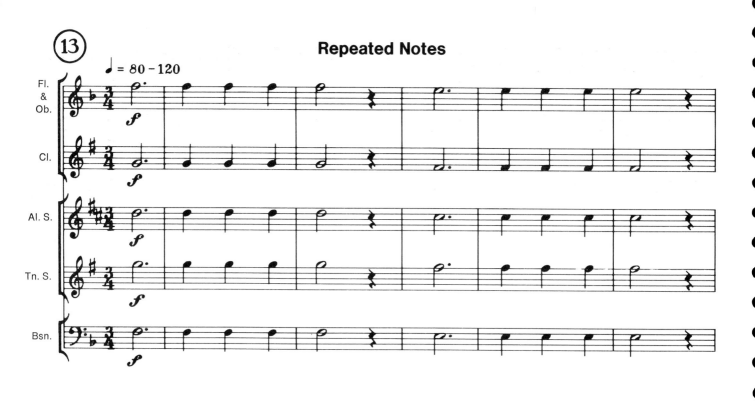

Practice same pattern starting with lower tonic and progressing upward.
Also, practice *ff – f – mf – mp – p – pp* .

Scale Etude

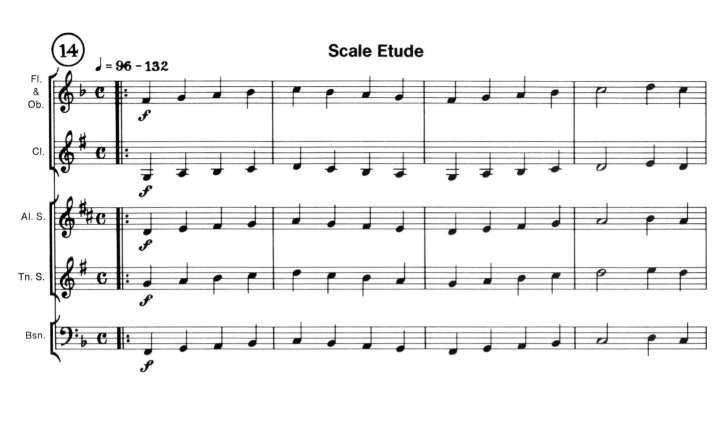

Etude

15

♩ = 108

Folk Song

French

44

So-Fa-Mi

Class Notes

18. Three-Part Round. Lovely Evening—Traditional

Review directions in the introduction on performance of rounds. Play with a smooth sustained tone, articulating carefully the first note under each slur. The final six measures provide an opportunity for soft clean articulation. Keep the volume of each of these notes constant—without accents, crescendo, or diminuendo.

(18) Three-Part Round

Lovely Evening

Traditional

Allegretto ♩ = 84 – 96

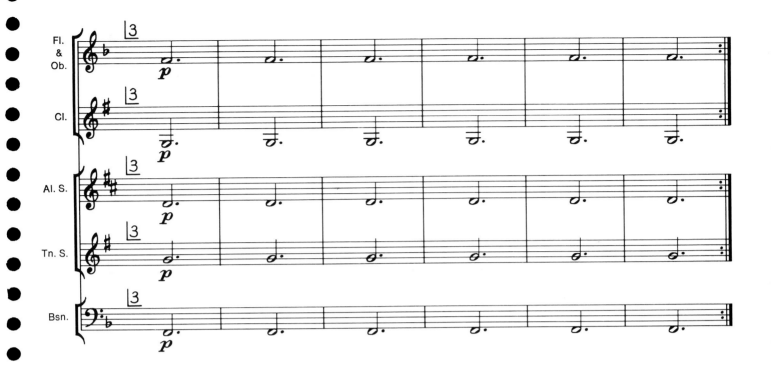

Class Notes

Class Notes

Basic Octave: Additional Notes

19. Preparatory Mechanism Studies for Left Hand

Some note patterns present more difficulty in finger co-ordination than others. Here are some for individual practice in preparation for exercise 20. If you have a particular problem in finger coordination, devise additional ones.

Repeat each pattern several times, starting slowly and gradually increasing speed. Play each pattern in different rhythms with notes of unequal length. Refer to the fingering chart for accuracy and for alternate fingerings. Make use of appropriate alternate fingerings.

(19) **Preparatory Mechanism Studies for Left Hand**

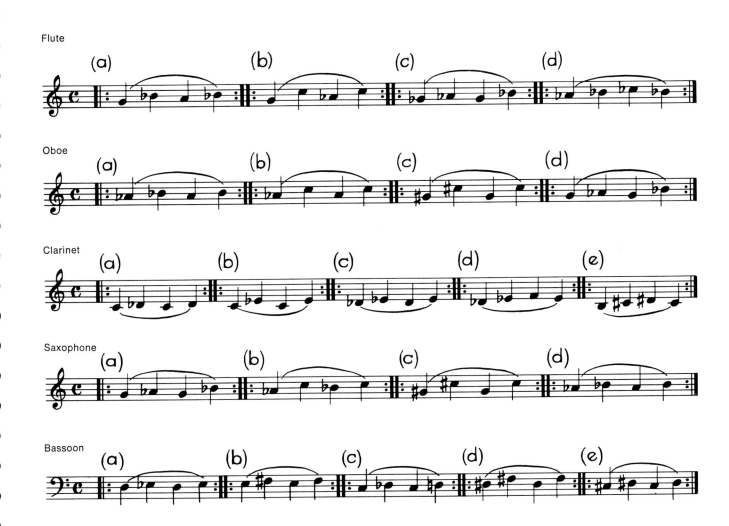

20. Left Hand Patterns

Practice exercise 1, patterns (a) through (i) using each of the note patterns of exercise 10 throughout. These patterns will establish the basic fingerings for all the notes in this range. Refer to the fingering chart for accuracy and for alternate fingerings. Some students find it helpful to establish the finger patterns silently before playing them on the instrument. *Review daily until the fingerings are firmly established.*

FLUTE: Continue to make use of both fingerings for B-flat—A-sharp.

OBOE: Practice first using fingering #28—000 400 for C-sharp, although on some instruments it is slightly out of tune. When this fingering is established, practice with fingering #27—1/2 23 456 C♯. After both fingerings are established choose the best fingering for a passage on the basis of facility, intonation, and tone quality.

Fingering #14—123 4x00, an alternate fingering for A-flat—G-sharp, is not used in this exercise. It is used for trills or when the little finger of the left hand is needed for another key on the note preceding or following.

CLARINET: Use fingering #16—T 120 4x00 for E-flat —D-sharp throughout this exercise. Fingering #17— T 123x 000 for this note is used primarily in chromatic passages, and never when the third finger covers the hole on the preceding or following note. Fingering #18 is a special situation fingering.

In combination III, fingering #22—T 000 4xy00, the chromatic fingering for F-sharp—G-flat, is the preferred fingering in patterns (a), (b), (d), (g), and the final note of (i).

SAXOPHONE: In combination II fingering #20—100 4C00, an alternate fingering for C may be used to become familiar with it. This fingering, primarily a trill fingering for B-C, has limited usefulness. It should not be used when the fourth finger is involved in the fingering of the note which precedes or follows it.

BASSOON: Notice that the first finger half-hole is used on F-sharp. Roll, do not slide, the finger down so that only half of the hole is covered. Practice using both fingerings #28 and #29—1/2 23 456 plus the F♯ key with the right thumb or right little finger. Both should be used with equal facility. Continue to use both fingerings #22 and #23 for E-flat—D-sharp. Be very careful of intonation with fingering #22.

DAILY STUDIES: Exercises 92 and 93 provide additional material for establishing these fingerings.

Left Hand Patterns Applied to Exercise 1

21. Preparatory Mechanism Studies for Right Hand

For individual study—repeat each pattern several times, starting slowly and gradually increasing speed. Play each pattern in different rhythms with notes of unequal length. Use all available alternate fingerings.

(21)   **Preparatory Mechanism Studies for Right Hand**

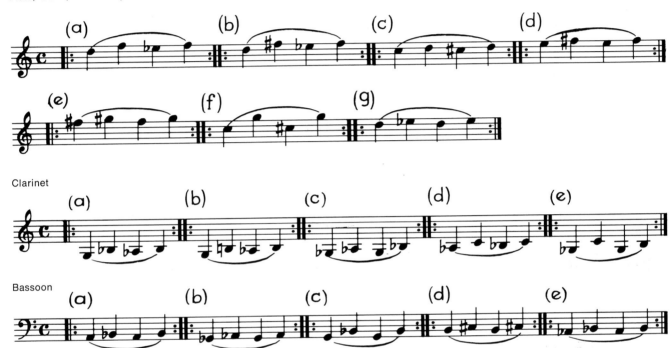

22. Right Hand Patterns

Practice exercise 2, patterns (a) through (i) using each of the note patterns of exercise 22 throughout. These patterns will establish the basic fingerings for all the notes in this range. Refer to the fingering chart for accuracy and for alternate fingerings. *Review daily until the fingerings are firmly established.*

FLUTE: Continue to use fingering #27—T 123 006 D♯ for F-sharp.

OBOE: Continue to use both fingerings for F-natural at the appropriate places. Develop equal facility in using either the left hand or right hand D-sharp key with the A 123 406 pattern.

CLARINET: Two fingerings for:

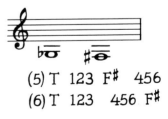

(5) T 123 F♯ 456
(6) T 123   456 F♯

The G-flat occurs in combination III. These two fingerings are identical except for the use of either the left or right little finger on the F-sharp key. In this note combination when the G-flat is preceded or followed by A-flat the *left* little finger must be used. Patterns (h) and (i) may use either the left or right little finger.

Three of the notes played with the little fingers may be played with either right or left. The G-sharp—A-flat may be played only with the right little finger:

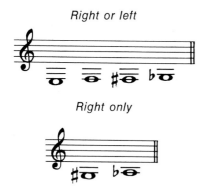

Right or left

Right only

As your study progresses you must read ahead and start a note pattern so that the G-sharp—A-flat can be played without sliding the little finger from another key. *Never play two consecutive notes with the same little finger.*

In combination III, use fingering #12—T 123 406x for C-flat (B-natural). This is the chromatic fingering for this note and is always used in a scale passage when C-flat or B-natural is preceded or followed by a B-flat. Use this fingering in patterns (a), (b), (d), (g), and for the final note of (i). The normal diatonic fingering is used in all other patterns.

SAXOPHONE: In combination V, fingering #29—T 123 406x, the chromatic fingering for F-sharp—G-flat, should be used in patterns (a), (b), (d), (f), and (g). This fingering is always used in scale passages when F-sharp is preceded or followed by an E-sharp or F-natural (or when G-flat is preceded or followed by an F-natural). Use of this fingering, and other alternate fingerings is determined by selecting the one which produces the smoothest technical facility. A basic rule in selecting fingering is: *never use the same finger in two different places on successive notes if an alternate fingering is available.*

BASSOON: Two fingerings for:

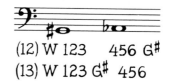

(12) W 123   456 G♯
(13) W 123 G♯   456

Learn to use these two fingerings with equal facility—they differ only in the use of the G-sharp key with either the right thumb or right little finger. The same two fingerings for G-flat—F-sharp are used in this octave, except the half-hole which is not used. Continue to use both for equal facility. Also continue the use of the two fingerings for B-flat—A-sharp. Selection of the proper fingering where alternates are available is based on which gives the best technical facility, intonation, and tone quality. *Never use the same finger in two different places on successive notes if an alternate fingering is available.*

㉒ Right Hand Patterns Applied to Exercise 2

Lourdes Hymn

Traditional

Symphony No. 8

Schubert

25. Slumber Song—Schubert

This melody makes use of notes in the fundamental octave previously learned. Play smoothly, with good tone quality, and in tune. Observe dynamics and nuances carefully. Be sure to articulate the first note under each slur.

Slumber Song

Schubert

Round

Four-Part Round

Hungary

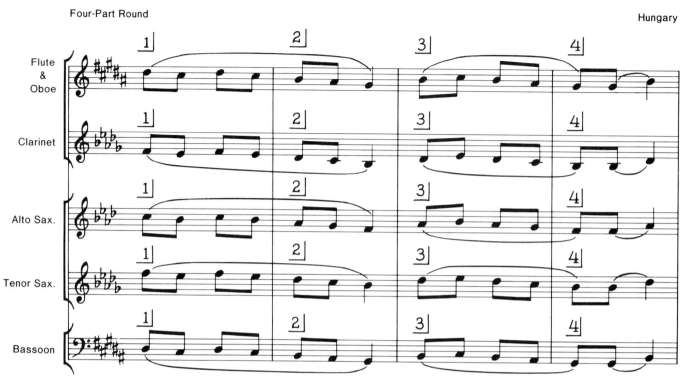

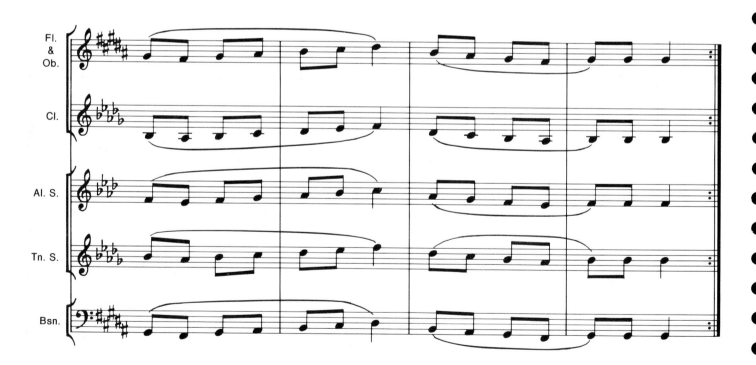

56

All Praise

Four-Part Round

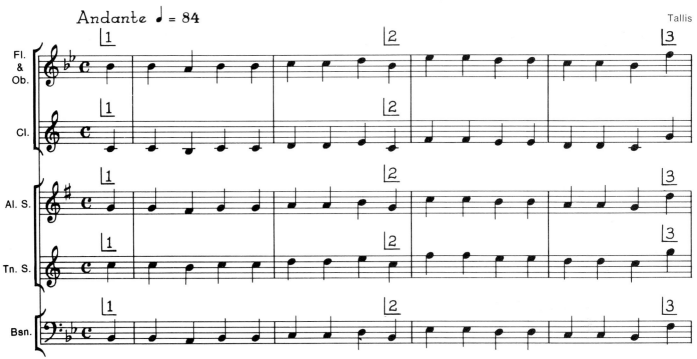

Tallis

Class Notes

Second Octave

28, 29, 30. Tone Studies

Observe dynamics and tempo markings carefully. The diminuendo and crescendo must be constant and gradual throughout the duration indicated. Changes of pitch must be done without a sudden change in loudness. Repeated practice of these exercises over a period of time will facilitate embouchure development and control. Take a breath at the end of any measure which is not slurred to the next, but use all your breath before taking another. Daily Studies 87, 88 and 89 apply to tonal development.

CLARINET: In addition to embouchure development and control, these exercises provide the foundation studies for the crossover from the low register *(chalameau)* to the upper register *(clarion)*. Before starting practice, check hand positions, especially that of the left thumb. Review directions and photographs in the introductory material. Fingering for the two slurred notes is identical except for the addition of the register key with the left thumb for the upper note. The register key is opened by a vertical movement of the first joint of the thumb. Do not slide the thumb. Practice these exercises until the upper notes can be played without a break in the continuity of tone, and without an accent. This can be easily accomplished if the embouchure formation is correct, and proper breath support is being used.

Tone Study: Fifths

Tone Study: Descrescendo

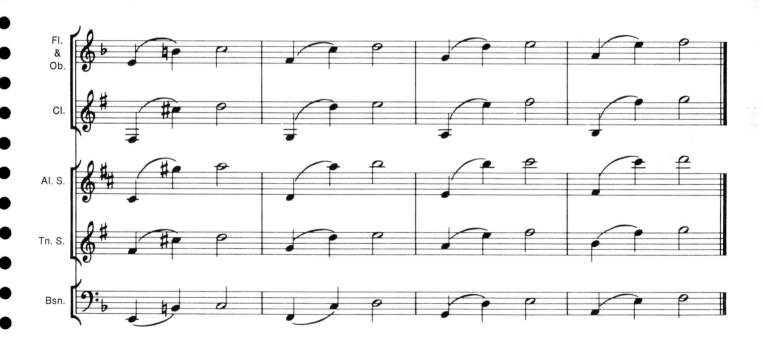

30 Tone Study: Long Tones, Crescendo, and Diminuendo

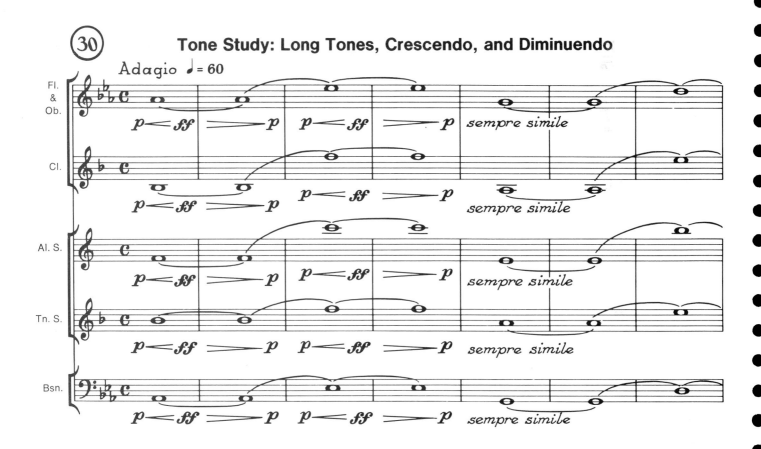

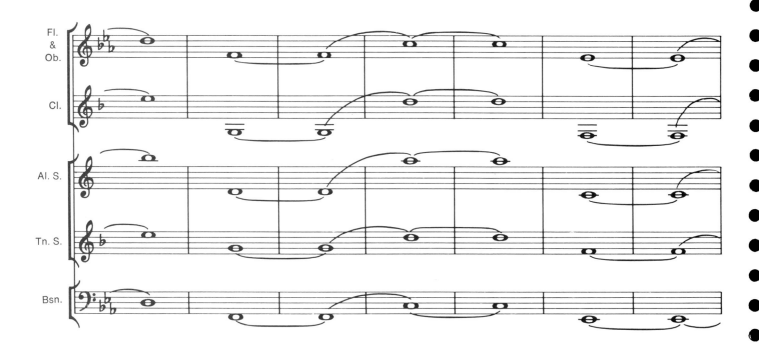

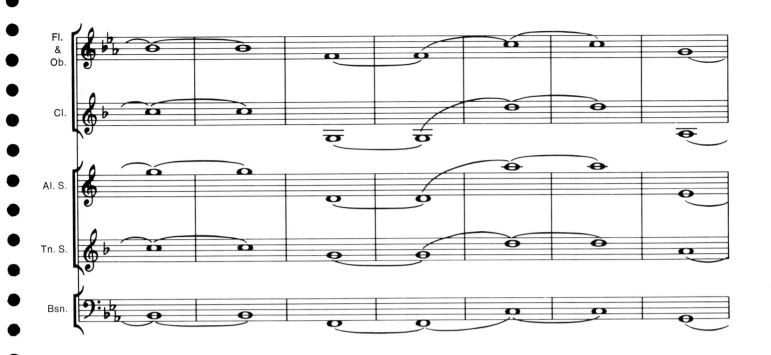

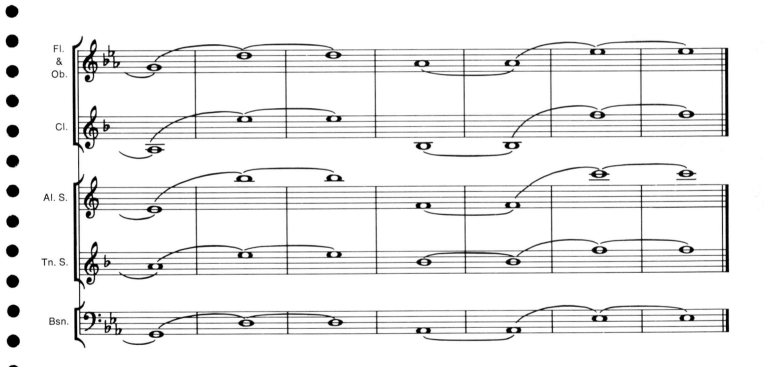

63

31. Right Hand Patterns—Second Octave

These finger patterns are identical with those in exercises 2 and 22, the flute, oboe, and saxophone an octave lower, the clarinet a twelfth higher, and the bassoon an octave higher. Fingerings for all notes are identical with those used in the earlier studies except for the minor alterations necessary to change the register in which they will sound. These changes are noted in the following paragraphs on the instruments. Verify doubtful fingerings with the fingering chart.

Some players will find it easier to establish these notes in a downward sequence. If you are insecure on the lower note, or the note doesn't respond easily, work downward from the top note until the starting note of the exercise responds easily.

Review daily until facility is established. Daily Studies 92 and 93 provide additional material for practicing these fingerings.

FLUTE: All fingerings are identical except that the first finger is down on the low D. Notes in this register are easily played utilizing, if necessary, one or more of the following: (1) slightly increase the size of the opening in the lips by drawing back the corners; (2) roll the flute slightly forward so that less of the blow hole is covered by the lower lip; (3) increase slightly the volume of air being used and decrease the pressure.

OBOE: All fingerings are identical except neither the half-hole nor octave key A is used. Decrease slightly the pressure of the lips around the reed and adjust breath support to achieve a volume of tone which is neither too loud nor too soft.

CLARINET: Observe that while the fingering patterns are identical with those of the earlier studies, the pitch of the notes is a twelfth higher. To the fingerings learned in exercises 2 and 22 add the register key, being extreme-

ly careful to maintain the proper hand positions, and paying particular attention to the position of the left thumb. Considerably less breath pressure is needed to produce these tones—adjust to achieve the proper tonal body and volume. No additional pressure of the lips around the mouthpiece is necessary. Avoid biting with the lower teeth. Do not change the position of the mouthpiece in the mouth. These notes will tend to be flat until the embouchure is developed. Generally it is better to leave the pitch flat temporarily rather than biting to bring it up, since this will hinder the development of a good embouchure.

SAXOPHONE: All fingerings are identical except for D-flat in pattern V. The octave key is not used for any of these notes. Slightly less pressure of the lower lip against the reed combined with a slight increase in breath support will make these lower notes respond easier. Avoid changing the position of the mouthpiece in the mouth.

BASSOON: Octave changes on the bassoon where the fingerings remain identical, as they do in these exercises, are controlled by the embouchure with the assistance of the whisper key (Key W, left thumb). Use of the whisper key is optional on G-flat, G-natural, and G-sharp —A-flat, and it must not be used for the higher notes. The need for this key varies with the instrument being used and with the player. Experiment for best results. Slightly more pressure of the lips around the reed is necessary for this upper octave. Avoid biting, and do not change the amount of reed taken into the mouth.

Exercises 31, 32, 33 and 34 are basic orientation to a second octave for each individual instrument. As such they cannot be played by a mixed ensemble of instruments.

Right Hand Patterns—Second Octave

FLUTE, OBOE, AND SAXOPHONE

Practice also using the following patterns of accidentals:

CLARINET

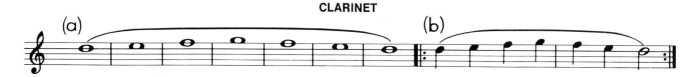

(a)   (b)

(c)   (d)

(e)   (f)

(g)   (h)

(i)   Practice also using the
                             following patterns of
                             accidentals:

I   II   III

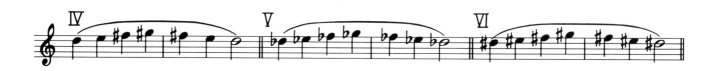

IV   V   VI

BASSOON

(a)

(b)

(c)

(d)

(e)

(f)

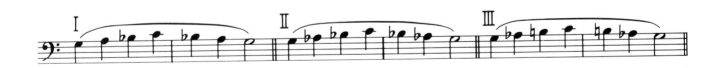

(g)

(h)

(i)

Practice also using the following patterns of accidentals:

I

II

III

IV

V

For individual study. Repeat each pattern several times, starting slowly and gradually increasing speed. Play each pattern in different rhythms with notes of unequal length. Choose fingerings carefully to avoid sliding fingers. Establish the use of available alternate fingerings.

Mechanism Studies: Right Hand, Second Octave

Flute, Oboe, and Saxophone

33. Left Hand Patterns—Second Octave

These finger patterns are identical with those in exercises 1 and 20, the flute, oboe, and saxophone an octave higher, the clarinet a twelfth higher, and the bassoon an octave higher. Fingerings for all notes are identical except for the minor alterations necessary to change the register in which they are being played. These alterations are noted in the following discussion. Verify doubtful fingerings with the fingering chart. Review daily until facility is established. Daily Studies 92 and 93 provide material for establishing these fingerings.

FLUTE: All fingerings are identical with those an octave lower. The octave in which a note will sound, where the fingerings are identical in two octaves, is controlled by the embouchure. If the lower octave speaks rather than the upper octave, the higher notes can be played by making one or more of the following adjustments: (1) slightly decrease the size of the opening in the lips, (2) roll the flute slightly inward so that more of the blow hole is covered by the lower lip, (3) direct the stream of air more across the blow hole, (4) increase breath support to get a more intense stream of air.

OBOE: All fingerings are identical with those an octave lower except for the use of the octave key. This exercise introduces the use of octave key B. Review the discussion of the use of the half-hole and octave key A in exercise 2.

Oboes are made with three different kinds of octave key mechanisms, and each is handled differently: (1) The automatic octave key model has a single octave key operated by the thumb, which automatically changes from one vent hole to another, an arrangement similar to that used on the saxophone; (2) The semiautomatic octave key model has the two octave keys, one operated by the thumb, the other by the first finger of the left hand. This model allows the thumb to be kept on its octave key while the side octave key is being used, the mechanism automatically closing the vent hole of the first when the second is opened: (3) Double octave key instruments have two independent octave keys which must be opened and closed independently by the thumb and first finger of the left hand. On this model when octave key B is used, the thumb must be removed from octave key A. Determine which model instrument you are playing.

Octave key B is operated by the first finger of the left hand and is used on the following notes:

For these notes the first finger also covers the tone hole. The key is opened by rolling the second joint of the finger upward, contacting the key between the first and second joints.

Careful practice will help establish the changes back and forth between the two octave keys. Practice slowly and carefully. A slightly increased pressure of the lips around the reed and increased breath support will help produce these notes clearly and in tune. Do not bite with the lower teeth.

CLARINET: All fingerings are identical with those a twelfth lower except for the use of the register key. Continue to pay close attention to hand position and finger placement. These notes need less breath pressure than those in the previous exercise. Adjust to achieve the best tone and volume. Avoid playing too loudly. A very slight increase in pressure of the lips around the mouthpiece will help intonation, but avoid biting with the lower teeth. These notes need less breath support than those in the previous exercise. Do not change the position of the mouthpiece in the mouth. If the notes do not respond, respond with difficulty, or are badly flat it is probable that the reed is too soft. Change to one which is harder.

SAXOPHONE: All fingerings are identical with those an octave lower with the addition of the octave key. A slight increase in the pressure of the lips around the mouthpiece will help the intonation, but avoid biting with the lower teeth. These notes need less breath support than those in the previous exercise. Do not change the position of the mouthpiece in the mouth. If the notes do not respond, respond with difficulty, or are badly flat it is probable that the reed is too soft.

BASSOON: The fingerings for E-natural, F, and F-sharp are different from those an octave lower. Practice first using these fingerings: E—(47), 103 D♯, (4)56; F—(49), 103(D♯), 450; F-sharp—(52), W 1/223, (D♯)400. If after some practice these do not respond properly, check the fingering chart for alternate fingerings. Note that in the fingerings for these notes the use of the D-sharp key with the little finger of the left hand is indicated as being optional, although some bassoonists feel that its use is mandatory. This key is used to increase tonal resonance, and should have little or no effect on the pitch. Use it if it makes your instrument respond better.

A slight increase in the pressure of the lips around the reed and an increase in breath support will be necessary to achieve good tone quality and intonation. Do not change the amount of reed taken into the mouth, and avoid biting the reed. If the notes do not respond, respond with difficulty, or are badly flat it is possible that the reed is too soft. Try one which is harder.

Left Hand Patterns—Second Octave
FLUTE, OBOE, AND SAXOPHONE

(a) (b)

(c) (d)

(e) (f)

(g) (h)

(i)

Practice also using the following patterns of accidentals:

I II III

IV V

CLARINET

Practice also using the following patterns of accidentals:

BASSOON

Practice also using the
following patterns of
accidentals:

For individual study. Follow directions given for
previous mechanism studies.

Mechanism Studies: Left Hand, Second Octave

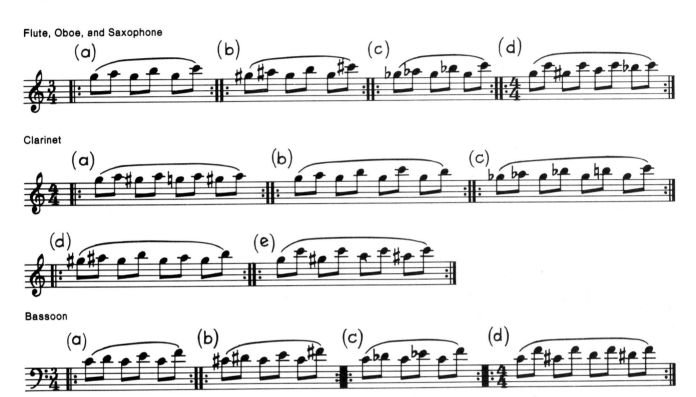

Repertoire

35, 36, 37. Compositions Using Wider Range

Play these compositions smoothly, matching quality and loudness of tones. Try to play phrases in one breath. Use normal articulation previously studied for first notes under slurs, and all notes not slurred. The adjustments in breath support for notes in the upper register may require an adjustment in the pressure of the tongue against the reed on oboe, clarinet, saxophone, and bassoon. Experiment with this relationship between breath support and tongue pressure until the notes which are tongued have a smooth clean attack without an accent. Avoid assisting each tongue movement with a simultaneous movement of the breathing muscles. This is not always a conscious action, and it is well to have someone else check for movement of the muscles while you are playing. Once the habit of involving breathing muscles with articulation is established it is very difficult to break.

ALTO SAXOPHONE: Beginning with exercise 35 the notation for alto saxophone is combined with that for bassoon on most of the remaining exercises, making use of the automatic transposition. To make the automatic transposition change to treble clef, add three sharps to the signature and read the notes as printed. The key signature for the alto saxophone is given beneath the staff at the beginning of each exercise. Appropriate changes in any accidentals must be made, and where the accidentals for alto saxophone differ from those printed for bassoon the correct accidental is printed beneath the note. While this procedure of automatic transposition may seem strange to those unfamiliar with it, only brief experience is necessary to use it with complete ease.

TENOR SAXOPHONE: Beginning with exercise 35 the notation for tenor saxophone is combined with that for clarinet on most of the remaining exercises. Some exercises are printed in octaves. Select the octave in the appropriate range.

Alma Mater

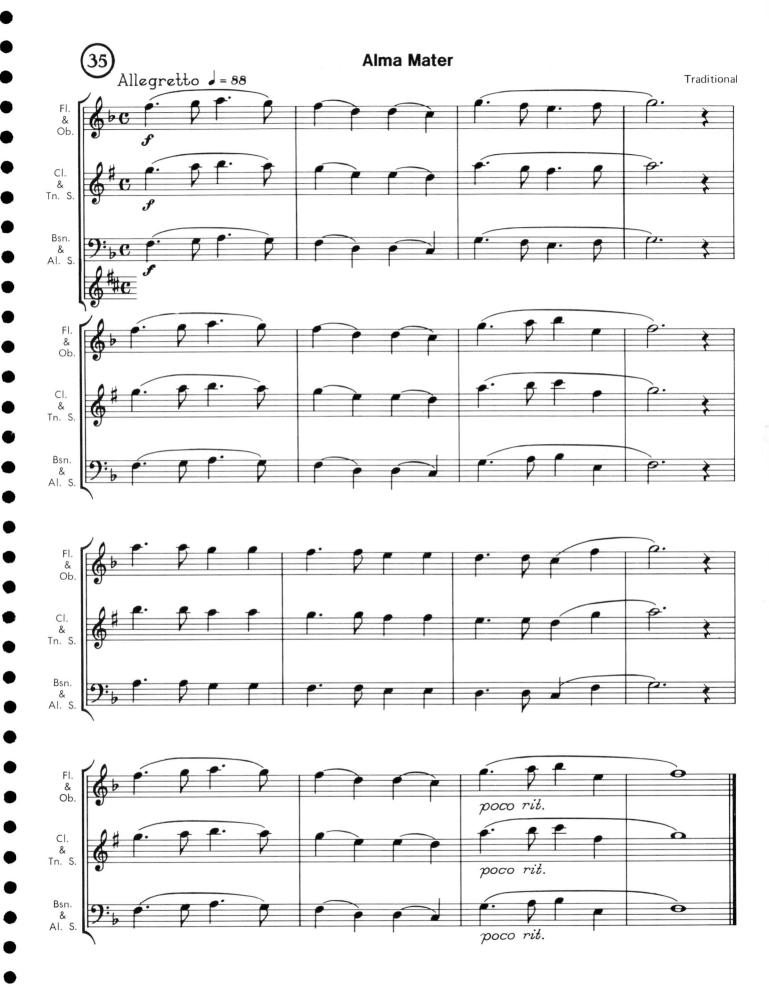

(36) Theme from Finale, First Symphony

Brahms

A Mighty Fortress

Class Notes

Crossing the Break

38. Studies

"Breaks" between registers occur on every woodwind instrument, although the term is most commonly used in connection with the clarinet. A break occurs at the point in the playing range where the vibrations of the air column producing the tone changes from the first partial to the second or third partial. The first break in the playing range of the instruments occurs between these two notes:

Flute-Oboe-Saxophone

Clarinet

Bassoon

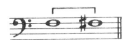

Fingerings for flute, oboe, saxophone, and bassoon starting with the upper note of the break are, with minor modifications, the same as those an octave lower. Clarinet fingerings are identical, except for the addition of the register key, with those a twelfth lower. The most important problem, aside from tone production, is to match the tone qualities of the notes below and above the break.

The following mechanism studies introduce the concept, and the next group of compositions provides musical application. Be sure fingerings are correct, and concentrate on matching and blending the tone quality above and below the break.

In exercise 38 (a) is directed specifically toward flute, (b) toward alto saxophone, (c) is for bassoon, and (d) for clarinet and tenor saxophone. Before practicing (c), tenor saxophone players should read the discussion of the articulated G-sharp key with exercise 43.

CLARINET: Aid to smooth crossing of the break. Inexperienced clarinetists sometimes have difficulty in crossing the break smoothly, primarily because of inaccurate finger placement. To achieve smoothness and accuracy the right hand portion of the upper note fingering is kept down. This does not effect the pitch of the throat tones, but actually increases their resonance.

The right hand portion of any of these notes:

may be kept down while playing any of these notes.

This technique is especially useful when crossing back and forth between notes in these two groups. When slurring upward from a throat tone the right hand portion of the next role is frequently prepared in advance as indicated in exercise 40, where the C fingering is prepared at the same time the A is played.

In the next few exercises, passages where right hand fingers may be kept down are bracketed. Acquire facility in using this technique and apply it throughout the remainder of the book. Additional material for developing this facility is found in Daily Study 92, middle octave of 12, 13, 14, and Daily Study 93, middle octave of 8-13.

Studies

Humming Song

Nicht schnell

Schumann

Fine

Melody

D.C.

82

In Arm der Liebe

㊵ Three-Part Round

Allegretto ♩ = 104

Beethoven

*) Prepare right hand portion of fingering for C at same time A is fingered.

**) Accidentals below staff are for alto saxophone using the automatic transposition.

Duet, Op. 59, No. 2

Pleyel

Andante cantabile M.M. ♪ = 92

One, Two, Three

Purcell

42 Three-Part Round
Allegro ♩ = 116

Development of Facility

43. Mechanism Study

This study will assist in the rapid development of finger coordination. Play each section at least four times. Practice slowly at first, gradually increasing speed as facility is developed. Practice both octaves where they appear in your part and are in range. Choose the proper fingerings and mark them in the music if necessary.

SPECIAL TECHNIQUE—ARTICULATED G-SHARP (OBOE, SAXOPHONE): An articulated G-sharp key is part of the keywork on oboes and saxophones. This mechanism automatically closes the G-sharp key when the fourth finger is down even though the little finger remains on the key. Taking advantage of this makes certain technical passages smoother and technically easier.

OBOE: Keep the little finger of the left hand down on the G-sharp key throughout the third measure of both (b) and (e). Select the preferred fingering for F and C in the patterns in which they occur.

CLARINET: Exercise 43 develops facility in the throat tones. It is essential that the position of the left hand remain in the standard guide position throughout. To help achieve this, the guide key E for the left little finger should be held down throughout, keeping the remaining fingers no more than a half-inch directly above the holes. In playing F-sharp to A in section (e) the first finger is rolled onto the A key. Do not slide.

SAXOPHONE: Exercise 43 provides an opportunity for the tenor saxophone to make use of the articulated G-sharp key, especially in section (e).

BASSOON: Review the two alternate fingerings for E-flat, A-flat, and F-sharp and select the best one to use in each instance. Where it is appropriate, practice using both fingerings.

Mechanism Studies

44-46. Development of Facility

The following group of compositions which are in a variety of styles provides an opportunity to make musical application of the techniques and facility developed thus far. Practice them for musical expression. Prepare all voice lines given for your instrument, including both octaves where they appear and are in range. Metronome markings are suggestive; use faster or slower tempi if desired.

SAXOPHONE: In these exercises the range is extended downward to the low B-natural on the instrument. For the lowest notes on the instrument do not change the basic embouchure formation, but lessen the pressure on the reed by relaxing the lower jaw and increasing slightly the velocity of breath through the instrument. In the finger patterns where the same little finger is used on different keys on successive notes keep the pressure of the finger down and make use of the rollers to change keys. Do not lift the finger to place it on the second key. Daily studies 92 and 93 provide additional material for establishing facility in this register.

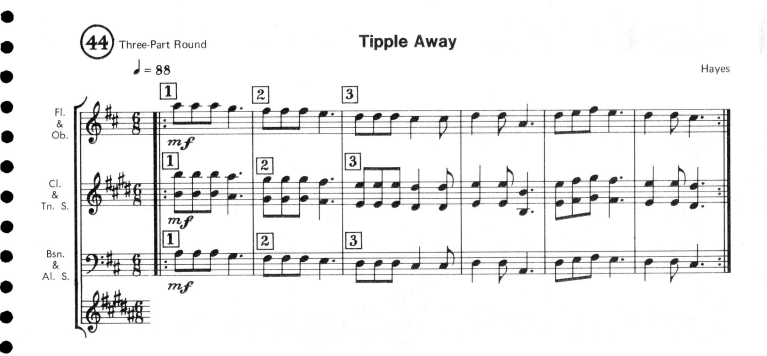

Duet

Klose

90

91

Duet, Op. 48, No. 3

Pleyel

Adagio espressivo ♩ = 60

Staccato Articulation

47-50. Staccato Articulation

The musical concept of a staccato note is that of a tone surrounded by silence. As a rule of thumb a staccato note is given half of its written value, with the other half replaced by a rest.

In the performance of staccato notes the placement and action of the tongue is the same as that learned for normal articulation, except that the tongue returns to the starting position to stop the tone. This can be visualized by putting a "t" on the end of the syllable used to start the tone: "tee—t"; "dee—t"; "too—t"; etc. Only in staccato articulation does the tongue stop the sound. Breath pressure against the tongue remains constant throughout a staccato passage. Avoid any movement of the breathing muscles to assist articulation.

Staccato articulation is best achieved at the beginning stage at a soft dynamic level. Establish the articulation in the following exercises softly, then at various louder levels. Use a variety of tempi, increasing speed as facility develops. Daily Studies 90 provides additional material for developing staccato articulation.

Clarinet should establish this articulation in the lower octaves and the tenor saxophone the upper octave first, then expand practice to the other range.

Repeated Notes

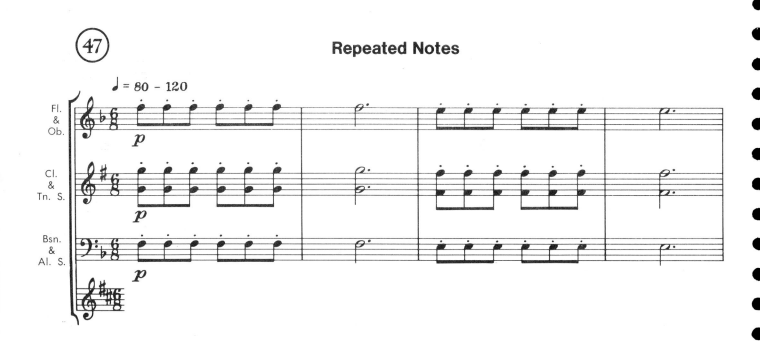

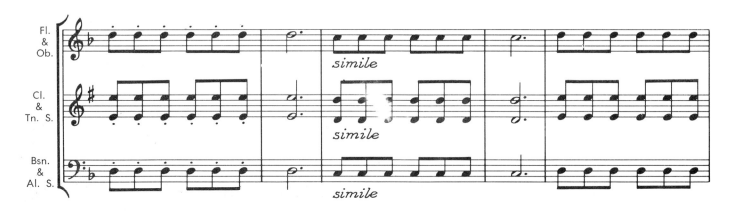

Scale Passages

Etude

Arban

Vivé La Compagnie

Traditional

Class Notes

Combined Slur and Staccato

51, 52. Combined Slur and Staccato

The most common musical use of the staccato on woodwind instruments is in patterns which combine slurred and staccato notes. This exercise should be practiced throughout with each of the four articulation patterns given and played at various speeds. These patterns are the most common for a four note grouping.

In order to accomplish the true staccato style, a brief silence must precede the first staccato tone following a slur. This is achieved by stopping the last note under the slur with the tongue. But remember that the tongue stops the last note *only* when the following note is staccato.

Class Notes

Etude

Klose

Practice the above also with these articulation patterns.

Special Technique

53. Bassoon Flick Keys

BASSOON FLICK KEYS: Flick keys (also called snip, tap, or flip keys) are used as an aid for producing good slurs to the following notes:

The left thumb flicks either key "a", "b" or "d" (on the fingering chart) as indicated above the notes so that the

key is open for just an instant at the beginning of the note. Don't leave the thumb on the key too long, or the note may not respond correctly. Flick keys are used:
1. Primarily for slurs at an interval of a fourth or more upward to the flick notes.
2. In certain situations the flick keys may be used in downward slurs to these notes.
3. To assist in getting a secure attack on the flicked notes where they are attacked directly. In this use the notes are attacked with the flick key pressed, and the key released immediately.

Practice the following intervals slowly to coordinate the use of the flick key:

a. Flick key "a"

b. Flick key "b":

54. Clarinet Preparation for High Register

The following study will prepare the clarinet student for playing notes in the high register. Use the normal fingering for the first of the three notes; add the register key for the second; lift the first finger and add the G-sharp key with the right little finger (except for C-sharp) for the third. Avoid biting for the high note. Keep breath support firm with a steady stream of air through the instrument. If the third note in the sequence does not respond after some practice, it is probable that the reed is too soft.

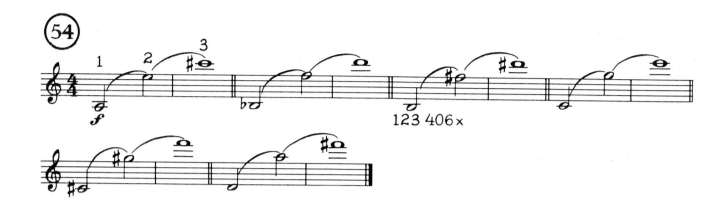

Upper Register

55-60. Upper Register

These exercises extend the upper playing range. Practice them slowly to establish the new fingerings, and increase the speed as facility develops. Watch intonation. Success in producing and controlling these notes does not come easily.

FLUTE: These notes can be played by using a smaller opening in the lips combined with a more intense stream of air. Rolling the instrument in so that the lower lip covers more of the blow hole helps make the most efficient use of the air stream.

As an aid in controlling the octave in which a note will sound, use the concept of changing the direction of the air stream by slight forward and backward movements of the lower jaw. Once a good embouchure is established the flutist may visualize:

The direction of the air more downward in the octave:

More across the hole in the octave:

More in an upward direction in the octave:

CLARINET: Establish the intervals in exercise 48 before practicing this series of exercises. A slight increase in pressure of the lips around the mouthpiece may be used for the high notes. Avoid biting. Observe that the little finger of the right hand is on the G-sharp key for all notes from D up. Without this key the notes will be flat.

Two fingerings for:

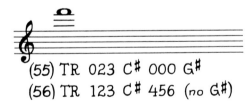

(55) TR 023 C♯ 000 G♯
(56) TR 123 C♯ 456 (no G♯)

Fingering 55 is the normal fingering used in most instances. Fingering 56 is a most useful alternate fingering which should be learned at this point, and is especially useful in the octave skip upward, and for sustaining the F at soft dynamic levels.

Use of the half-hole. In order to make a perfect slur from a note in the clarion register to one in the upper register it is necessary to make use of the half-hole technique. In this, the first finger is rolled down to cover half of the first hole instead of being taken entirely off the hole for the upper note. The second and third measures of exercise 56 are an excellent example since the second note under each slur can be played by simply rolling the first finger to the half-hole position and adding the G-sharp key with the right little finger. The half-hole is used only for slurs up into notes of this register. It is not used for descending slurs, or when the upper note is tongued.

SAXOPHONE: The notes in this register from D up are fingered with side keys. In playing these notes keep the hands as close to the guide position as possible. The D key is directly beneath the knuckle of the first finger of the left hand and is opened with a slight downward movement of the knuckles of the hand. The E-flat key is opened with the first finger below the first joint. The high F key lies directly beneath and is operated by the *second* finger straightened slightly and moved downward. The high E key is played by the right first finger and requires a slight rotation of the wrist to reach. It contacts the finger between the kunckle and first joint. Items 1-5 and 22-24 of Daily Study 92 and items 16-21 of Daily Study 93 provide material for establishing these fingerings.

BASSOON: While the previous range is not extended to any appreciable degree, these exercises provide additional study in intervals, especially the octave which is an important part of bassoon technique. The upper range may be extended even higher through use of the daily studies. Avoid changing the position of the reed in the mouth for interval skips. Control the pitch changes by pressure of the lips around the reed.

The upper notes in daily exercises 91, 92, and 93 are especially useful in gaining facility in this register. Ranges used in exercises 87, 88, 89, and 90 may also be extended.

F Major Scale

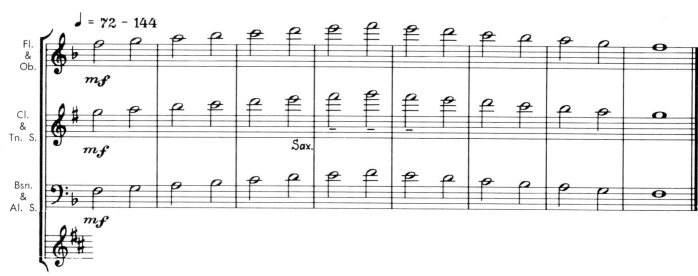

Class Notes

Ascending and Descending Sixths

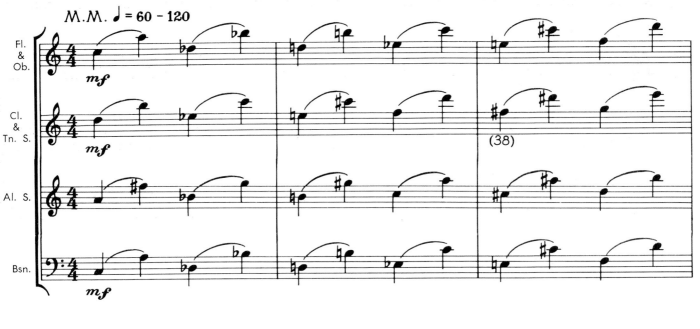

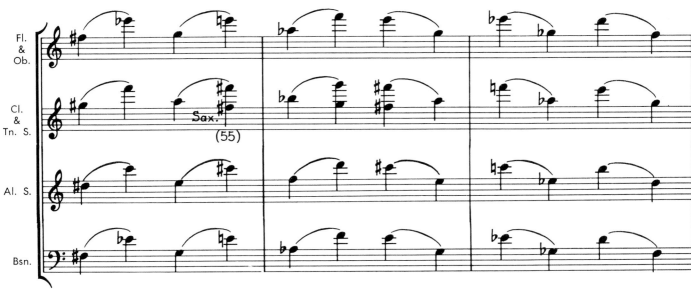

Practice also *p - mp - f - ff*

Class Notes

Octaves

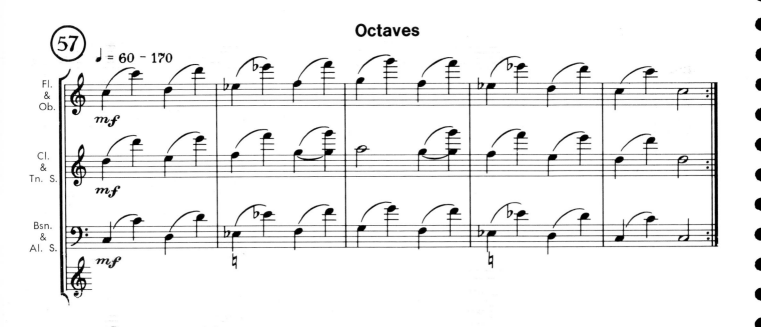

Class Notes

Ballade

Third Movement, Trio Op. 11

Beethoven

Chromatics

61-65. Chromatics

Chromatics on woodwind instruments are a special problem since careful choice of fingerings must be made in order to achieve smoothness and facility. For the most part regular fingerings are used in chromatic passages, however each instrument has certain notes which have preferred alternate fingerings for chromatic progressions. Remember the basic rule for selection of fingering: *The same finger is never used in two different places for consecutive notes if an alternate fingering is available.*

Following are the notes on each instrument which have particular fingerings for use in chromatic passages, together with the number from the fingering chart of the fingering to be used:

Flute:

Oboe:

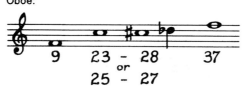

Clarinet:

Saxophone:

Bassoon:

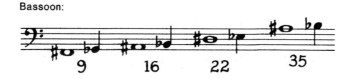

Special Technique

61. Introduction of Chromatic Fingerings

The mechanism studies which follow for individual practice will establish the most commonly used chromatic fingerings. Use the fingerings which are indicated by fingering chart number. Play each exercise at least four times before going on to the next.

Chromatic Octave Scales

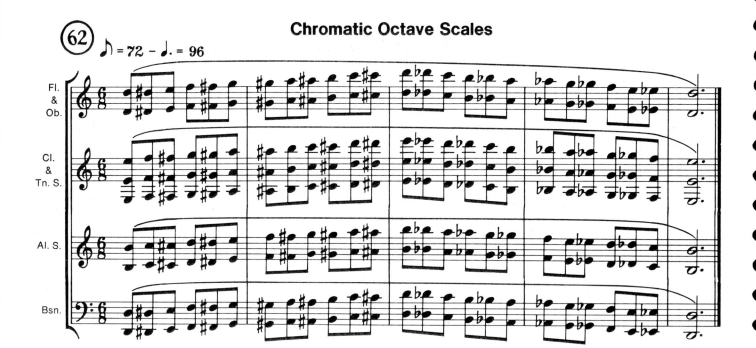

Class Notes

(63) Chromatic Patterns Ascending and Descending

♪ = 72 to ♩ = 112

For articulation, practice also exercise 63 throughout with each of these patterns:

A   B   C   D

Etude

(64) ♪ = 116

120

Duet, Op. 80, No. 36

Küffner

123

Repertoire

Ich bitt' dich

Beethoven

Nachtigallen

Three-Part Round

Haydn

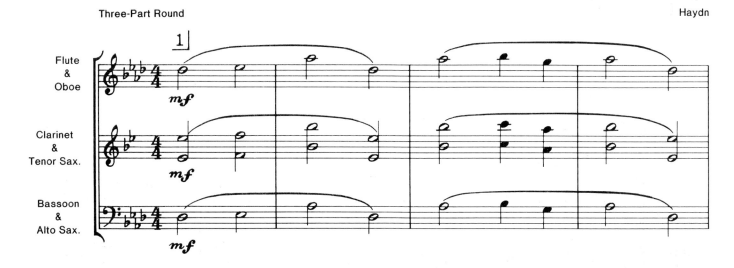

Three-Part Round

Nay Prithee, John

Purcell

Giocoso ♩ = 112

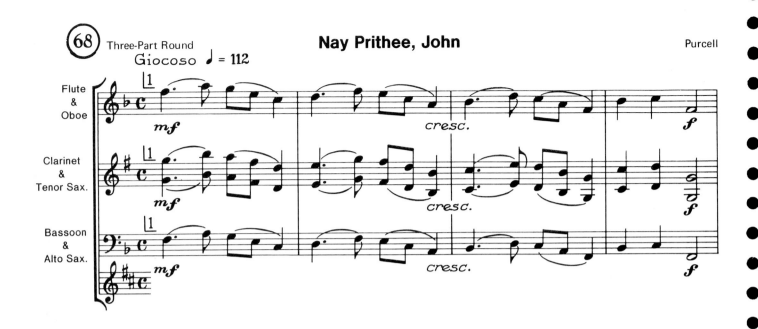

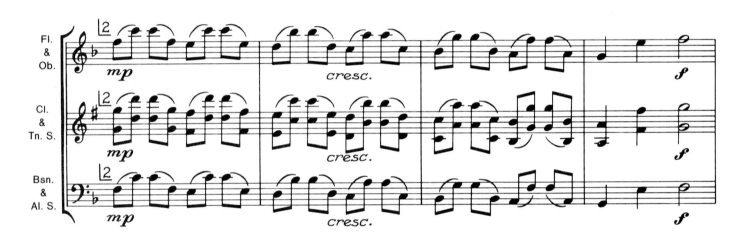

Trills

69-70. Trills

Trills on woodwind instruments are executed either with the standard fingerings for both notes or with special trill fingerings if the standard fingerings are awkward. Because of the mechanics of the keyworks of the woodwinds many trills are possible only with these special trill fingerings, some of which may compromise to some extent the intonation and/or tone quality of the upper note. Such fingerings cannot be tolerated when played slowly, but are satisfactory when played at a normal trill speed. There are dozens of such fingerings on each instrument. When a trill is encountered which cannot be played with standard fingerings, a special trill fingering chart such as those in the author's *Guide to Teaching Woodwinds* should be consulted.

Developing Trills. Trills must be played smoothly and with both notes of equal intensity. Trill with finger movements from the knuckle. Avoid movements of the hand, wrist, or forearm. Practice each trill in exercise 63 in the rhythmic pattern suggested at various tempi. A composite fingering for both notes of the trill is given beneath the notes. The trill is made with the fingers and/or keys circled.

TRILL PATTERN:

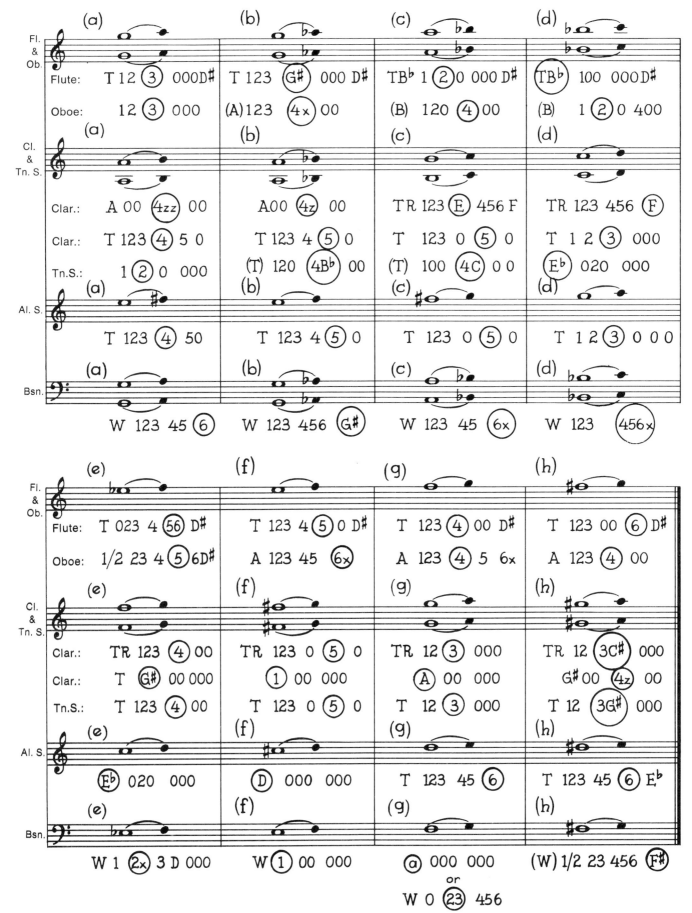

Duet

Klose

Class Notes

Legato Articulation

71-75. Legato Articulation

Legato articulation is used where notes must be articulated, but where a minimum space or amount of silence is wanted between them. Tongue position and action is much the same as in normal and staccato articulation, except that the tongue breaks the column of air only momentarily. The force with which it touches the reed or the back of the teeth on the flute is much less than in the previous types of articulation.

The amount of pressure of the tongue against the reed (or teeth) determines the hardness of the attack. The amount of wind pressure against the tongue determines the loudness of the attack. With the proper proportion of tongue pressure and wind pressure a great variety of attacks can be produced. A skilled woodwind player can duplicate the entire range of sounds produced by string players using the various bow strokes. Exercises 66-70 provide material for developing legato articulation in musical contexts.

To produce legato articulation follow the recommendations of your instructor, or use the following directions:

FLUTE: The tip of the tongue touches lightly the back of the upper teeth at the gum line. Use a tongue action similar to that of pronouncing the letter "D."

OBOE: Touch tip of reed lightly, use tongue action similar to that in pronouncing the letter "D."

CLARINET: With tongue in position in the small "V" shaped pocket, use tongue action similar to that in pronouncing "doo," using a very light pressure of the tongue against the reed. Be sure the tongue is not flat on the reed. This articulation is best established using the lower octaves of the exercises, then applied to the upper octaves.

SAXOPHONE: With tongue in position in the small "V" shaped pocket, use tongue action similar to that in pronouncing "doo" using a very light pressure of the tongue against the reed. Be sure that the tongue is not flat on the reed. Tenor saxophone should establish this articulation on the upper octaves of the following exercises before applying it to the lower octaves.

BASSOON: Touch the tip of the reed lightly, using tongue action similar to that in pronouncing the letter "D."

Repeated Notes

(71)

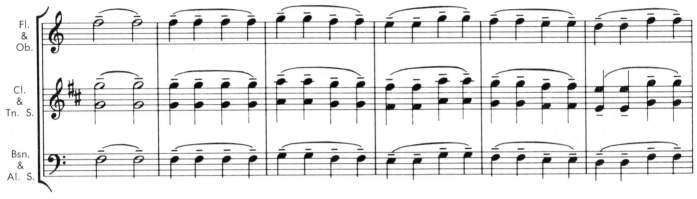

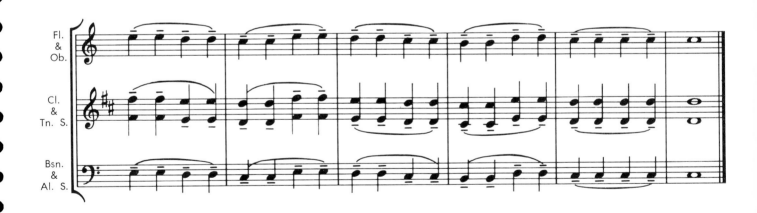

72 Three-Part Round **Great Tom Is Cast** Lawes

73 Three-Part Round **The Silver Swan** Gibbons

134

Duet, Op. 80, No. 25

Küffner

(75) Trio

Second Movement from Symphony No. 7

Allegretto ♩ = 76

Beethoven

136

Class Notes

Special Technique

76. Flute Compound Tonguing

Double and triple tonguing is commonly used in flute playing, as it is on brass instruments, although its use is rare on the other woodwinds. Double or triple tonguing is used for rapidly moving passages where normal single tonguing is difficult or impossible.

Double tonguing is executed by using the syllables "tu-ku" (or "ti-ki" or "doo-goo"). The first syllable is pronounced with the tongue in the same position as for single tonguing and the second syllable articulated with the tongue striking the palate to stop the flow of air. The two syllables flow together in rapid succession, and is used where the notes are grouped in twos.

To develop a feeling for this articulation, practice the following studies starting slowly and gradually increasing speed. Be sure all notes are the same length and rhythmically even.

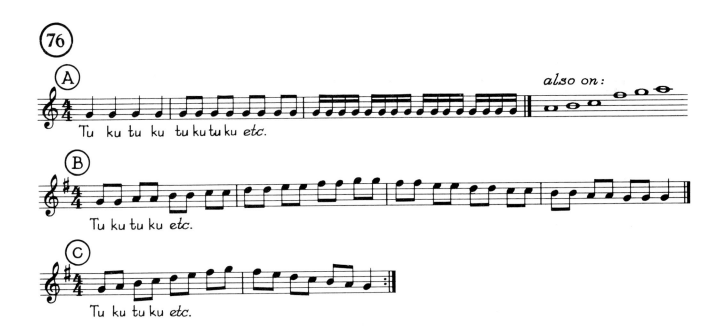

Triple tonguing is used for rapidly moving passages where the notes are grouped in threes. Making use of the same syllables as double tonguing, triple tonguing is executed with "tu-ki-tu," "tik-ki-ti," or "doo-goo-doo." An alternate procedure is to use the double tonguing syllables, but group the notes in threes: "tu-ku-tu," "ku-tu-ku," "tu-ku-tu," "ku-tu-ku," etc.

Practice the following exercises slowly and gradually increase speed as control is developed.

Additional practice: Double Tonguing—exercises 48, 49, and 51. Apply rhythmic patterns of examples B and C to scales in exercise 90.

Triple Tonguing—exercises 47, 50 and 63. Apply rhythmic patterns of examples E and F to scales in exercise 90.

Class Notes

Repertoire

77 Four-Part Round   **To Maelzel**

Allegretto ♩ = 72   Beethoven

Menuet from Anna Magdalena's Notebook

J.S. Bach

Oboe Sonata in C minor

Handel

80 Duet

Dance from Anna Magdalena's Notebook

J.S. Bach

148

Vibrato

81-82. Vibrato: An Introduction

The almost universal use of vibrato on woodwind instruments makes it something the instrumental teacher must understand and be prepared to teach. Vibrato should not be introduced until the player is well into the intermediate or advanced stage of performance—it is not a part of beginning performance techniques. There are considerable differences of opinion on how a vibrato should be produced on woodwind instruments, how fast the vibrato should be, and how and when it should be used. For a complete discussion of vibrato see the author's *Guide to Teaching Woodwinds.*

This presentation of vibrato is for the purpose of introducing the concept and presenting a method of developing a tasteful vibrato on woodwind instruments. This is only one approach; your instructor might have another which he prefers.

There are two basic methods of producing vibrato:

1. *Diaphragmatic vibrato* is produced by increasing and decreasing the wind pressure against the embouchure by controlled motions of the diaphragm and abdominal muscles. This kind of vibrato may be used on any of the woodwind instruments, but is almost universally used on flute.

2. *Jaw vibrato* is produced by slight up and down motions of the lower jaw producing changes in the pressure of the lips against the reed; or in the flute, slight changes in the direction of wind across the embouchure hole.

Recommendations: Flute—diaphragmatic; Oboe—diaphragmatic preferred; Clarinet—jaw; Saxophone—jaw; Bassoon—diaphragmatic preferred, although jaw vibrato is widely used.

Developing a Vibrato: Practice exercise 77 A-B. With the metronome set at ♩=60 practice with one fluctuation of the tone to each beat. Increase metronome speed little by little up to 120 beats per minute, keeping one complete movement of the tone per beat.

After the tone fluctuations come easily at this speed, move the metronome back to sixty beats per minute. Practice successive vibratos of one, two, three, and four fluctuations per beat. Do the same thing gradually increasing the metronome tempo to 100 beats per minute. The standard speed when a vibrato is fully developed and under control is four pulsations per beat at metronomic speeds of 72 to 104.

In exercise 82 use vibrato on part A only. For further practice on vibrato use the rounds "Lovely Evening" #18, "The Silver Swan" #73, and "When Jesus Wept" #59.

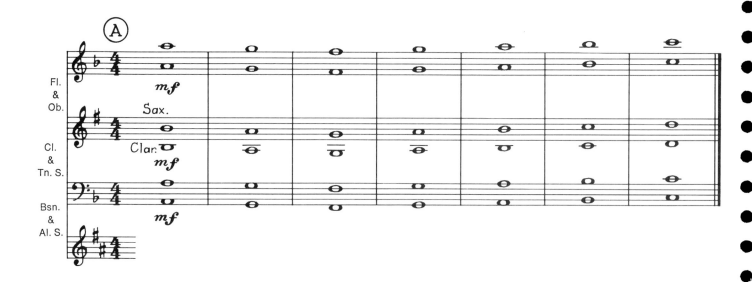

Class Notes

Duet

Andantino

Klose

153

Repertoire

83 Duet   **Siciliano, Op. 59, No. 1**

Pleyel

(84) **Ich Weiss Nicht**

Four-Part Round

Brahms

156

Class Notes

Viva Tutti

Italian

85 Trio

Allegro ♩ = 120

158

159

Trio

Menuet

Allegro ♩ = 132

Mozart

Class Notes

Daily Studies: Flute and Oboe

These studies are in unison for all instruments and may be played together. They are separated by instrument for convenient use.

Begin practice each day with appropriate excerpts from these studies. Alternate keys and articulation patterns from day to day so that all are covered. In the early portion of study a limited number of these will be within the ability of the average student. New examples should be added as rapidly as facility develops. Regular use of these studies will establish both tone control and technical facility over a wide range of the instrument.

87 Long Tones

Practice using one full breath for each note; then one breath for each two notes. Do the same for each of the scales given in exercise 90. Be sure that the pitch remains constant throughout the dynamic range.

88 Octaves for Tonal Development

Practice using a full tone; then at various dynamic levels. Watch intonation carefully.

89 Fifths for Tonal Development

Be sure that the slurs are perfect and that the pitch remains constant throughout the dynamic range.

Flute and Oboe

90 **Major and Minor Scales**

Use both octaves if they are in your playing range. Play at different dynamic levels matching each tone. Establish a key at a very slow tempo, increasing speed as facility increases. Use various rhythm and articulation patterns. The natural and harmonic scales may be used in addition to the melodic minor given here.

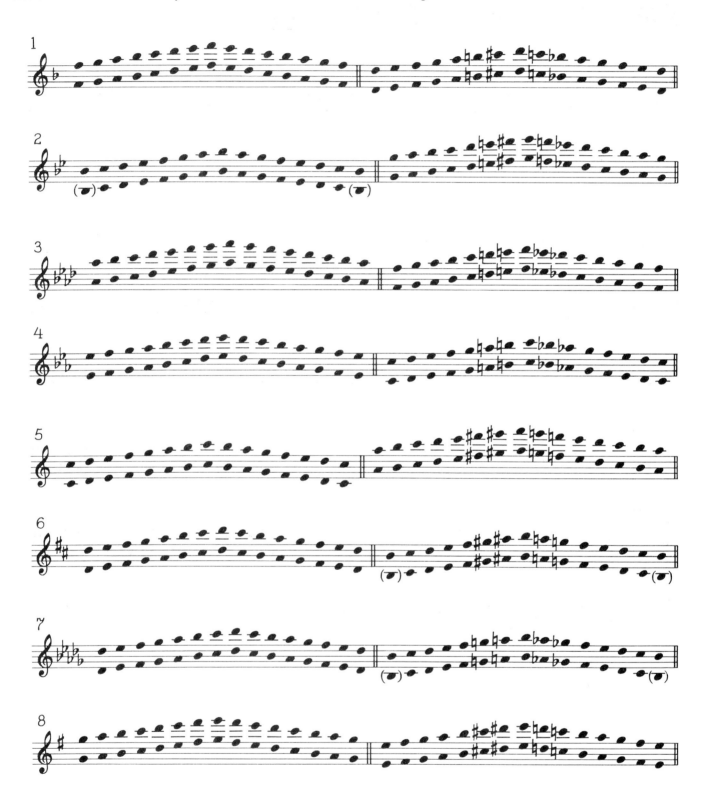

Suggested forms for practicing scales. Make use of: (1) long slurs, (2) articulating each note, and (3) combinations of tongued and slurred notes.

etc. then down

etc.

(91) Arpeggios

A standard pattern to be used on all the arpeggios is established on two fundamental pitches. Use this pattern for all the chords indicated. Repeat each measure three times before continuing to the final note. Stop on any fundamental if the following pattern goes out of your playing range. Make use of various articulation patterns. Begin the patterns on chord roots in various octaves of your instrument.

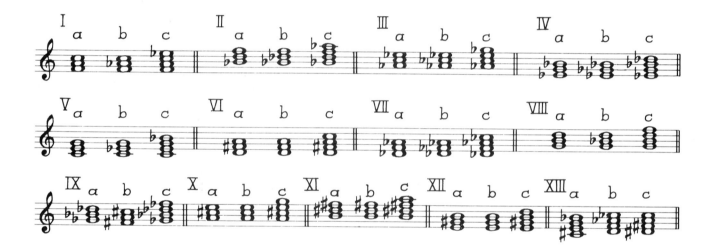

92 **Interval Studies—Seconds**

A basic pattern is indicated to be used on all the intervals given. Establish the pattern slowly, gradually increasing speed as facility develops. Practice all octaves that are in your playing range.

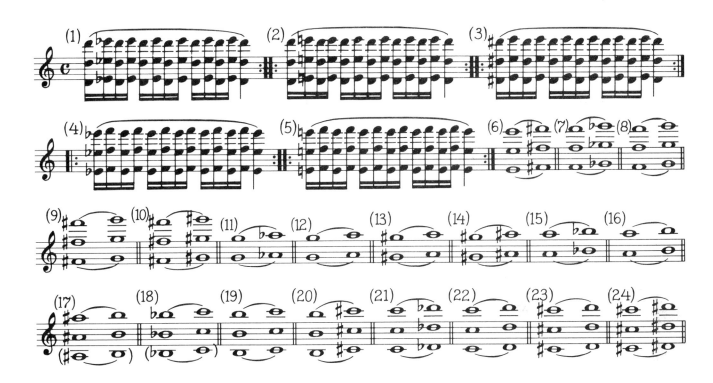

93 **Interval Studies—Thirds**

Use the same pattern on all intervals, gradually increasing speed. Practice all octaves that are in your range. Choose the best fingering where alternatives are available.

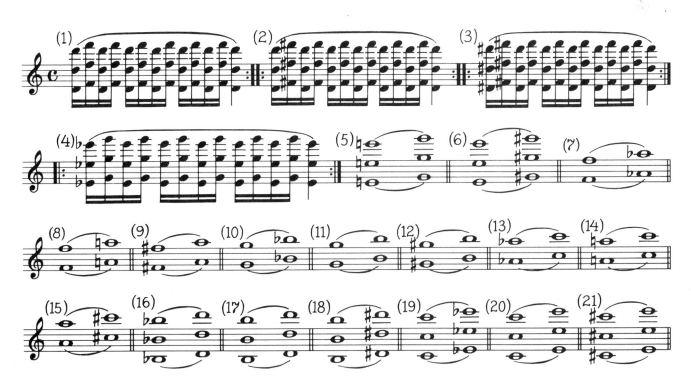

Daily Studies: Clarinet and Tenor Saxophone

These studies are in unison for all instruments and may be played together. They are separated by instrument for convenient use.

Begin practice each day with appropriate excerpts from these studies. Alternate keys and articulation patterns from day to day so that all are covered. In the early portion of study a limited number of these will be within the ability of the average student. New examples should be added as rapidly as facility develops. Regular use of these studies will establish both tone control and technical facility over a wide range of the instrument.

(87) Long Tones

Practice using one full breath for each note; then one breath for each two notes. Do the same for each of the scales given in exercise 90. Be sure that the pitch remains constant throughout the dynamic range.

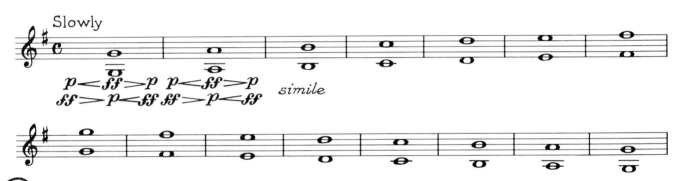

(88) Octaves for Tonal Development

Practice using a full tone; then at various dynamic levels. Watch intonation carefully.

(89) Twelfths (Fifths) for Tonal Development

Be sure that the slurs are perfect and that the pitch remains constant throughout the dynamic range.

Clarinet

Tenor Saxophone

90 **Major and Minor Scales**

Use both octaves if they are in your playing range. Play at different dynamic levels matching each tone. Establish a key at a very slow tempo, increasing speed as facility increases. Use various rhythm and articulation patterns. The natural and harmonic scales may be used in addition to the melodic minor given here.

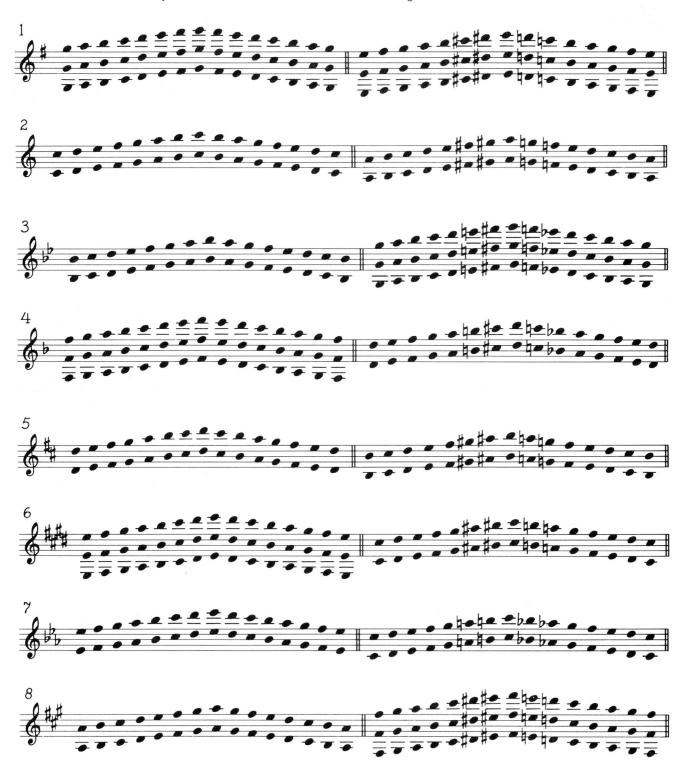

Suggested forms for practicing scales. Make use of: (1) long slurs, (2) articulating each note, and (3) combinations of tongued and slurred notes.

(91) Arpeggios

A standard pattern to be used on all the arpeggios is established on two fundamental pitches. Use this pattern for all the chords indicated. Repeat each measure three times before continuing to the final note. Stop on any fundamental if the following pattern goes out of your playing range. Make use of various articulation patterns. Begin the patterns on chord roots in various octaves of your instrument.

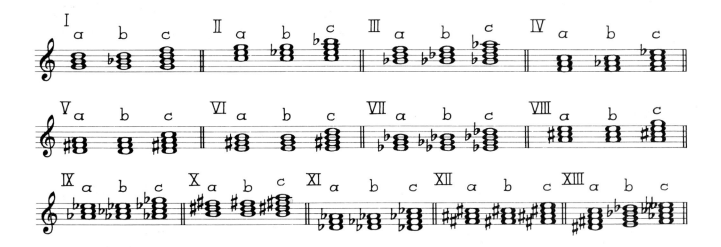

(92) **Interval Studies—Seconds**

A basic pattern is indicated to be used on all the intervals given. Establish the pattern slowly, gradually increasing speed as facility develops. Practice all octaves that are in your playing range.

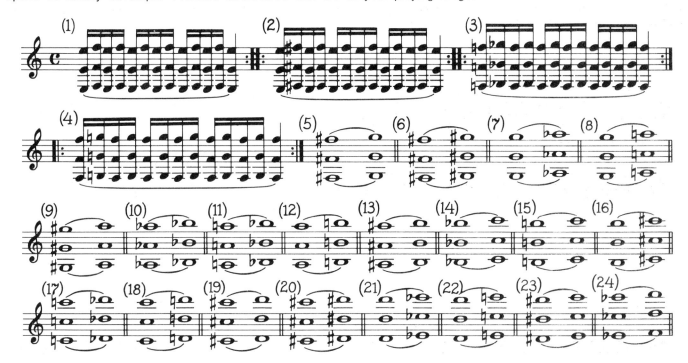

(93) **Interval Studies—Thirds**

Use the same pattern on all intervals, gradually increasing speed. Practice all octaves that are in your range. Choose the best fingering where alternatives are available.

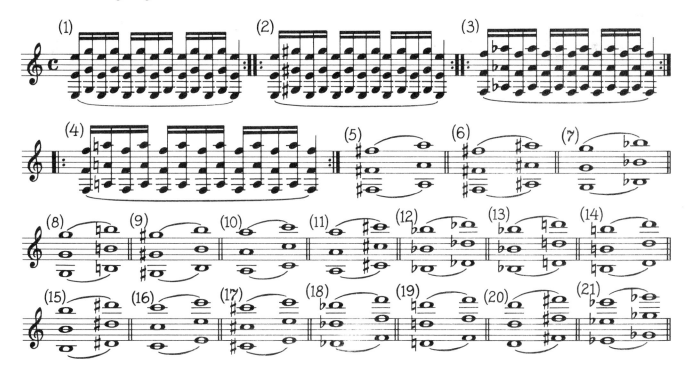

Class Notes

Daily Studies: Alto Saxophone

These studies are in unison for all instruments and may be played together. They are separated by instrument for convenient use.

Begin practice each day with appropriate excerpts from these studies. Alternate keys and articulation patterns from day to day so that all are covered. In the early portion of study a limited number of these will be within the ability of the average student. New examples should be added as rapidly as facility develops. Regular use of these studies will establish both tone control and technical facility over a wide range of the instrument.

(87) Long Tones

Practice using one full breath for each note; then one breath for each two notes. Do the same for each of the scales given in exercise 90. Be sure that the pitch remains constant throughout the dynamic range.

(88) Octaves for Tonal Development

Practice using a full tone; then at various dynamic levels. Watch intonation carefully.

(89) Fifths for Tonal Development

Be sure that the slurs are perfect and that the pitch remains constant throughout the dynamic range.

Alto Saxophone

(90) Major and Minor Scales

Use both octaves if they are in your playing range. Play at different dynamic levels matching each tone. Establish a key at a very slow tempo increasing speed as facility increases. Use various rhythm and articulation patterns. The natural and harmonic scales may be used in addition to the melodic minor given here.

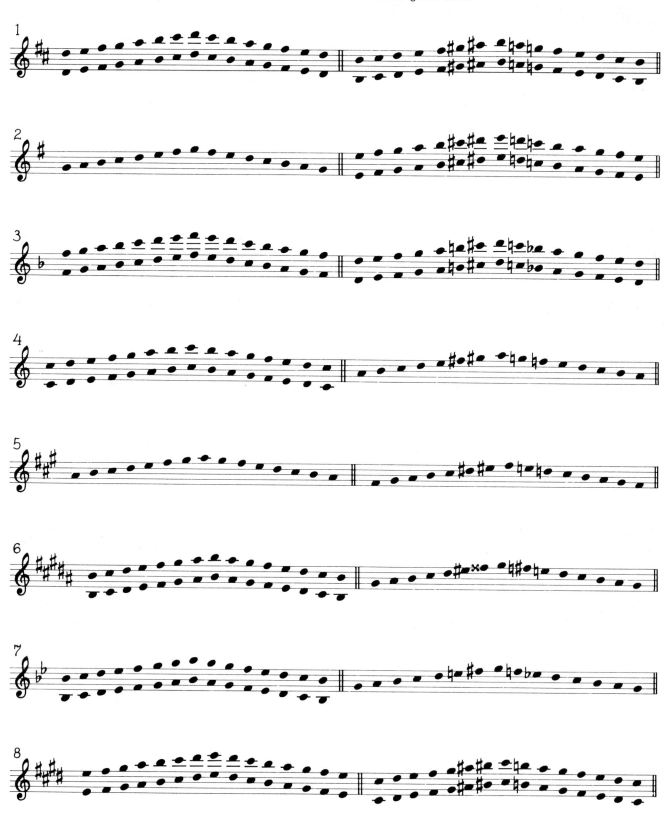

Suggested forms for practicing scales. Make use of: (1) long slurs, (2) articulating each note, and (3) combinations of tongued and slurred notes.

etc. then down

etc.

91 Arpeggios

A standard pattern to be used on all the arpeggios is established on two fundamental pitches. Use this pattern for all the chords indicated. Repeat each measure three times before continuing to the final note. Stop on any fundamental if the following pattern goes out of your playing range. Make use of various articulation patterns. Begin the patterns on chord roots in various octaves of your instrument.

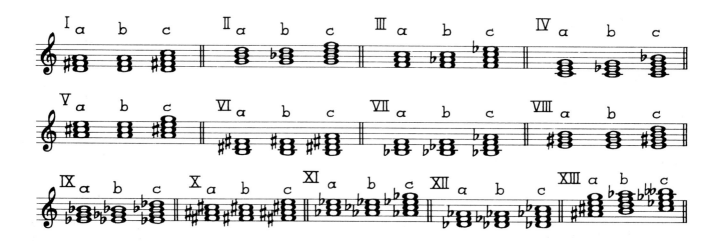

92 **Interval Studies—Seconds**

A basic pattern is indicated to be used on all the intervals given. Establish the pattern slowly, gradually increasing speed as facility develops. Practice all octaves that are in your playing range.

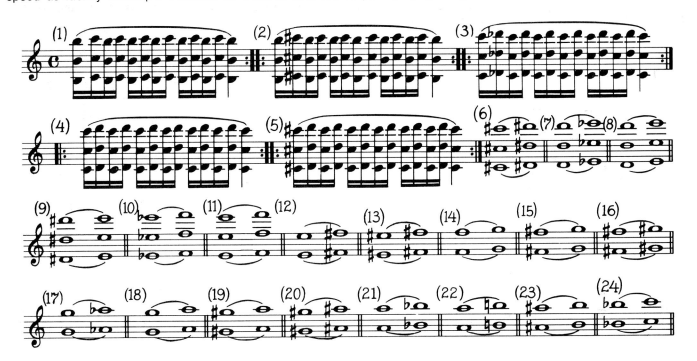

93 **Interval Studies—Thirds**

Use the same pattern on all intervals, gradually increasing speed. Practice all octaves that are in your range. Choose the best fingering where alternatives are available.

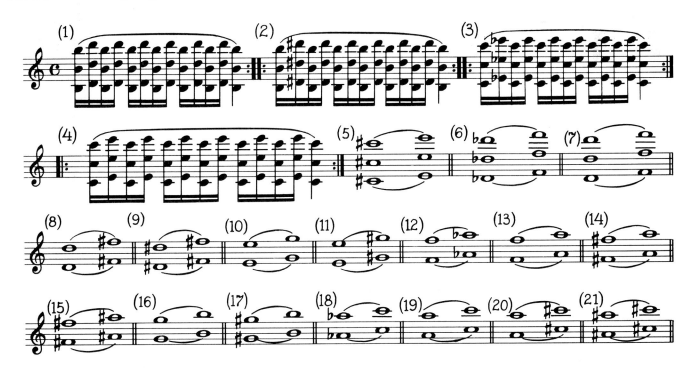

Daily Studies: Bassoon

These studies are in unison for all instruments and may be played together. They are separated by instrument for convenient use.

Begin practice each day with appropriate excerpts from these studies. Alternate keys and articulation patterns from day to day so that all are covered. In the early portion of study a limited number of these will be within the ability of the average student. New examples should be added as rapidly as facility develops. Regular use of these studies will establish both tone control and technical facility over a wide range of the instrument.

87 Long Tones

Practice using one full breath for each note; then one breath for each two notes. Do the same for each of the scales given in exercise 90. Be sure that the pitch remains constant throughout the dynamic range.

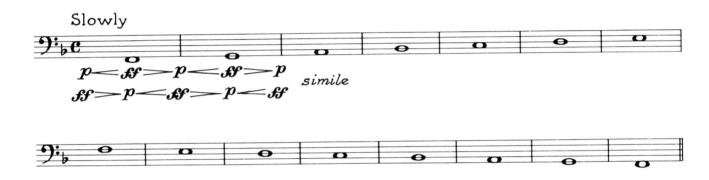

88 Octaves for Tonal Development

Practice using a full tone; then at various dynamic levels. Watch intonation carefully.

89 Fifths for Tonal Development

Be sure that the slurs are perfect and that the pitch remains constant throughout the dynamic range.

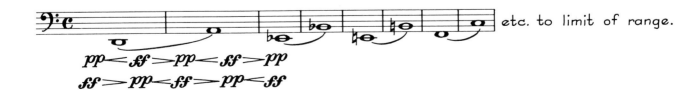

(90) Major and Minor Scales

Use both octaves if they are in your playing range. Play at different dynamic levels matching each tone. Establish a key at a very slow tempo, increasing speed as facility increases. Use various rhythm and articulation patterns. The natural and harmonic scales may be used in addition to the melodic minor given here.

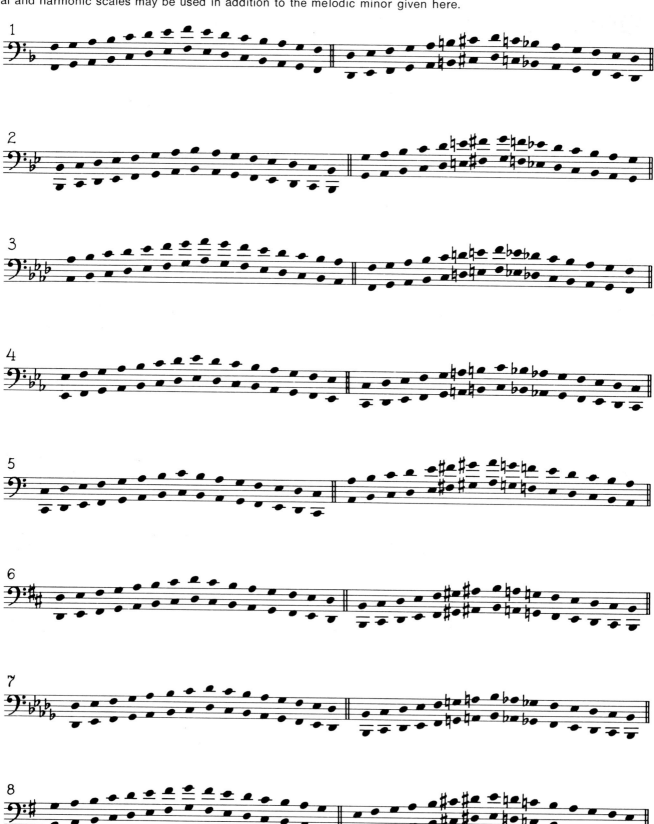

Suggested forms for practicing scales. Make use of: (1) long slurs, (2) articulating each note, and (3) combinations of tongued and slurred notes.

Bassoon

(91) Arpeggios

A standard pattern to be used on all the arpeggios is established on two fundamental pitches. Use this pattern for all the chords indicated. Repeat each measure three times before continuing to the final note. Stop on any fundamental if the following pattern goes out of your playing range. Make use of various articulation patterns. Begin the patterns on chord roots in various octaves of your instrument.

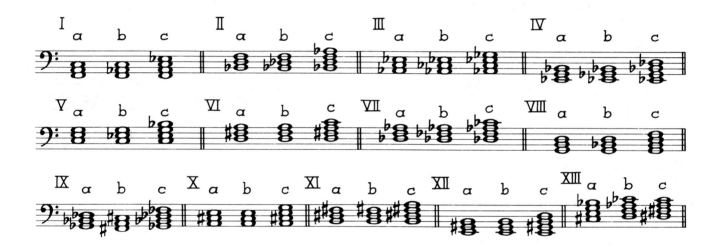

92 **Interval Studies—Seconds**

A basic pattern is indicated to be used on all the intervals given. Establish the pattern slowly, gradually increasing speed as facility develops. Practice all octaves that are in your playing range.

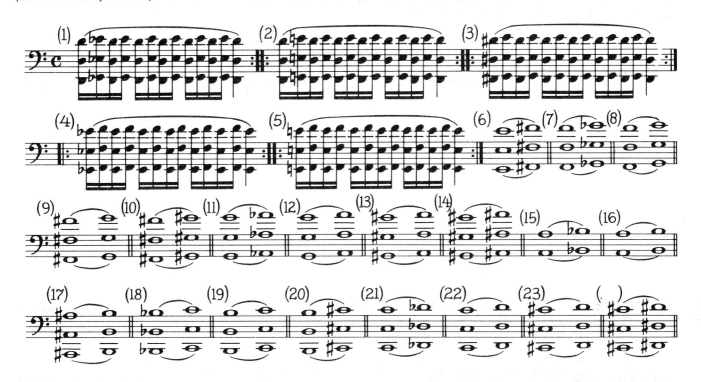

93 **Interval Studies—Thirds**

Use the same pattern on all intervals, gradually increasing speed. Practice all octaves that are in your range. Choose the best fingering where alternatives are available.

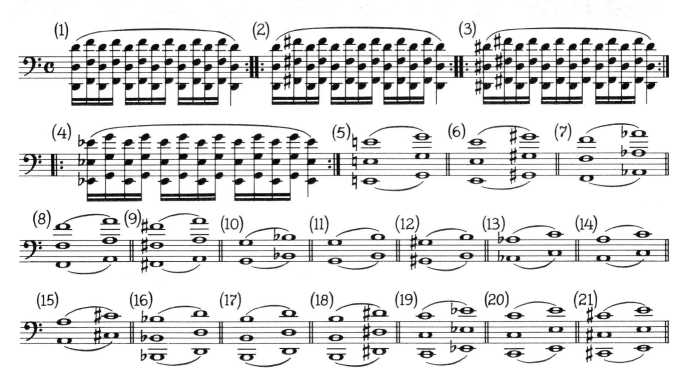

Study and Achievement Questions

I. *General Questions Applicable to All Instruments*

   1. Identify parts of the instrument.
   2. Demonstrate correct procedure for assembly and disassembly of the instrument.
   3. Explain and demonstrate holding position, hand position, and guide position.
   4. Explain and demonstrate correct embouchure formation.
   5. Demonstrate and discuss tuning of the instrument.
   6. Discuss daily routine care of the instrument.
   7. Demonstrate chromatic fingerings by playing exercise 62, or by joining with a fellow student in playing the duet exercise 65.
   8. Discuss the three types of articulation presented, and demonstrate each on the instrument.
   9. Discuss breathing and breath support on the instrument, including differences in the various registers of the instrument.
   10. What is the open note on each instrument? The lowest note?
   11. Write on a staff the notes which have alternate fingerings and discuss the uses of each.
   12. How are trills executed on woodwinds? Demonstrate a trill fingering using standard fingerings for both notes and one which uses a special trill fingering.
   13. What are the two basic methods of producing vibrato on woodwinds? Which can be used (or is preferable) on each instrument? Play a melody using vibrato.
   14. Select and perform a composition from the book which demonstrates tone quality, phrasing, and musical attainment.
   15. Select and perform a composition from the book which best demonstrates the technical facility which you have acquired.
   16. Select and perform at least one composition for solo instrument with piano accompaniment.

II. *Flute*

   1. Discuss and demonstrate embouchure adjustments made to achieve the best tone in the various registers of the instrument.
   2. If a flute student is expending his breath too rapidly and having to breathe too often, what remedial measures may be taken?
   3. Discuss and demonstrate placement of the tongue for articulation.
   4. Describe the use of the right little finger on the D-sharp key.
   5. Other woodwind instruments have octave or register keys to control register in which the notes will sound. When fingerings are identical, how is the octave in which they will sound controlled on the flute? Demonstrate.
   6. Teach a fellow student to play the preliminary tone production on the head joint alone.
   7. What is compound tonguing? Describe and illustrate how it is executed and used.

III. *Oboe*

   1. Discuss and demonstrate the use of the half-hole and the two octave keys, indicating on what notes each is used.
   2. Third-space C and C-sharp each have two fingerings. Demonstrate these and give the basic factors which determine their choice.
   3. Unlike other instruments, oboists frequently have a surplus of air, which may cause some discomfort. What would you tell a student to correct this condition?
   4. Describe and demonstrate placement of the tongue for articulation.
   5. What is an articulated G-sharp key? Point out how it works and demonstrate its use.
   6. Describe the three octave-key systems available on oboes and how each must be used. Identify and illustrate the use of the system on the instrument you are playing.

IV. *Clarinet*

   1. Describe and demonstrate placement of the tongue on the reed for articulation.
   2. Discuss and demonstrate embouchure adjustments needed to achieve the best tone in the various registers of the instrument.
   3. Identify the various registers of the instrument according to their commonly accepted names, and indicate notes which fall into each.
   4. Demonstrate and discuss placement of the reed and ligature on the mouthpiece. Discover the effect on playing when the reed is over the tip of the mouthpiece; when it is too far down from the tip.
   5. Demonstrate the correct position of the left hand when playing the throat tones. What suggestion would you have to help a student establish the correct position?

6. What basic rule would you make for the selections of the proper sequence of fingerings?
7. Demonstrate the correct playing position of the left thumb; the correct holding position of the right thumb.
8. Describe and demonstrate the procedure for teaching students to play in the clarion register once the chalameau register is established.
9. What is the "break" on the clarinet? Discuss and demonstrate a useful technique for crossing over the break.
10. Under what conditions and for what purpose is the half-hole used in the clarinet? Demonstrate how it is used.
11. On the staff write the notes which can be played with either the right or left little fingers; those which can be played only with the right little finger. What determines the choice of fingerings for these notes?

V. *Saxophone*

1. Describe and demonstrate placement of the tongue on the reed for articulation. Compare placement for the alto and tenor saxophones.
2. Demonstrate the correct playing position of the left thumb and its action in operating the octave key. Also demonstrate the correct placement of the right thumb.
3. Demonstrate and discuss placement of the reed and ligature on the mouthpiece and the effects of improper alignment; placement too far from the tip of the mouthpiece and too far over the tip.
4. Describe and demonstrate use of the little fingers in playing a passage involving a series of notes in the lowest register of the instrument.
5. What is an articulated G-sharp key? Point out how it works and demonstrate its use.
6. Demonstrate the correct placement, use, and movement of the first and fourth fingers in playing a passage involving a series of notes in the highest register of the instrument.
7. Between what two notes does the break occur? Discuss the problems of matching the tone quality across the break. Are there alternate fingerings available to solve some problems?

VI. *Bassoon*

1. A good bassoonist is frequently described as a person who is "all thumbs." Discuss the possible reasons for this statement.
2. How is the octave in which the instrument sounds controlled when the fingering is identical in both?
3. What basic rule would you make for the selection of the proper sequence of fingerings?
4. Discuss and demonstrate embouchure adjustments made to achieve the best tone in various registers of the instrument.
5. Describe and demonstrate placement of the tongue for articulation.
6. Discuss and demonstrate the use of the whisper key and the half-hole.
7. What are "flick" keys? Describe and demonstrate their use.

Fingering Charts

FLUTE FINGERING CHART

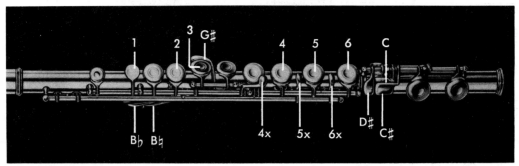

Photo courtesy C. G. Conn Ltd.

x—indicates keys operated by fingers normally covering holes. When these keys are used the hole operated by that finger remains open.

T—Left thumb on either lever except where indicated otherwise. Normal position is on the B-natural lever.

The D-sharp key is down on all notes except Low C, C-sharp, the two D-naturals, and the highest B-flat, B-natural, and C.

Fingerings are numbered and referred to in the text over notes to indicate special usage.

			Left Hand	Right Hand
C		1.	T 123	456 C
C♯		2.	T 123	456 C♯
D		3.	T 123	456
D♯		4.	T 123	456 D♯
E		5.	T 123	450 D♯
F		6.	T 123	400 D♯
F♯		7.	T 123	006 D♯
		8.	T 123	050 D♯
G		9.	T 123	000 D♯

			Left Hand	Right Hand
G♯		10.	T 123 G♯	000 D♯
A		11.	T 120	000 D♯
A♯		12.	T 100	400 D♯
		13.	TB♭ 100	000 D♯
		14.	T 100	4X00 D♯
B		15.	TB 100	000 D♯
C		16.	100	000 D♯
		17.	(T) 123	456 C
C♯		18.	000	000 D♯
		19.	123	456 C♯
		20.	T 023	456 C♯
D		21.	T 023	456
		22.	(TB) 100	05X0 D♯
D♯		23.	T 023	456 D♯
		24.	(T) 100	006X D♯

190

Note	Staff	No.	Left Hand	Right Hand
E		25.	T 123	450 D♯
F		26.	T 123	400 D♯
F♯		27. 28.	T 123 T 123	006 D♯ 050 D♯
G		29.	T 123	000 D♯
G♯		30.	T 123 G♯	000 D♯
A		31.	T 120	000 D♯
A♯		32. 33. 34.	T 100 TB♭ 100 T 100	400 D♯ 000 D♯ 4X00 D♯
B		35.	TB 100	000 D♯
C		36. 37.	100 T 023	000 D♯ 450 D♯
C♯		38. 39. 40.	000 T 023 003	000 D♯ 05(6) D♯ 456 D♯
D		41. 42.	T 023 T 123	000 D♯ 000 D♯

Note	Staff	No.	Left Hand	Right Hand
D♯		43. 44. 45.	T 123 G♯ T (1)23 T (1)23 G♯	456 D♯ 456 D♯ 05x0 D♯
E		46. 47. 48.	T 120 T 120 T 103	450 D♯ 456x D♯ 456 D♯
F		49. 50. 51.	T 103 T 103 TB 000	400 D♯ or C 406 D♯ 000 D♯
F♯		52. 53. 54.	TB 103 TB 103 T 123	006 (C♯) 050 D♯ 400 D♯
G		55. 56.	123 T 023	000 D♯ 456 D♯
G♯		57. 58. 59.	023 G♯ 023 G♯ T 023 G♯	000 D♯ 056 D♯ 450 D♯
A		60. 61. 62.	T 020 (G♯) T 020 T 103	400 (D♯) 406 C♯ 45x6x D♯
A♯		63. 64. 65.	T 000 T 000 TB 103	45x0 (D♯) 406x (D♯) 05x6
B		66. 67.	TB 103 TB 103	006x (D♯) 05x6x D♯ or C
C		68. 69. 70. 71. 72.	123 G♯ (T) 123 G♯ 123 123 (G♯) 123 G♯	400 (C) 406 C 45x6 (C) 406x (C) 456

OBOE FINGERING CHART

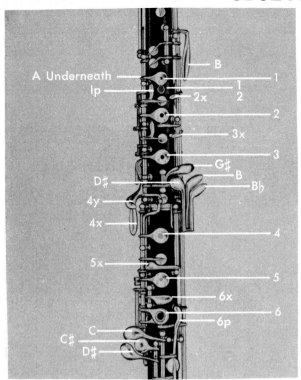

Photo courtesy C. G. Conn Ltd.

( )—Keys in parenthesis indicate its use in that fingering is optional, depending on intonation and resonance on a particular instrument.

x, y—indicate keys operated by fingers normally covering holes. When these keys are used the hole operated by that finger remains open.

Fingerings are numbered and referred to in the text under notes to indicate special usage.

			Left Hand	Right Hand
B♭		1.	123 B♭	456 C
B		2.	123 B	456 C
C		3.	123	456 C
C♯		4.	123	456 C♯
D		5.	123	456
D♯		6. 7.	123 123 D♯	456 D♯ 456
E		8.	123	450

			Left Hand	Right Hand
F		9. 10.	123 123 (D♯)	456x 406 (D♯)
F♯		11.	123	400
G		12.	123	000
G♯		13. 14.	123 C♯ 123	000 4x00
A		15.	120	000
A♯		16. 17. 18.	120 103 G♯ 103	400 000 4x00
B		19. 20. 21. 22.	100 11p00 103 B♭ 120 B	000 400 456 C 456 C

			Left Hand	Right Hand
C		23.	100	400
		24.	020	000
		25.	103	456 C
		26.	½23	456 C
C#		27.	½23	456 C#
		28.	000	400
		29.	103	456 C#
		30.	103x	000
D		31.	½23	456
		32.	100	45x0
		33.	12x0	400
D#		34.	½23	456 D#
		35.	½23 D#	456
E		36.	A 123	450
F		37.	A 123	456x
		38.	A 123 (D#)	406 (D#)
F#		39.	A 123	400
G		40.	A 123	000
G#		41.	A 123 G#	000
		42.	A 123	4x00
A		43.	B 120	000
A#		44.	B 120	400
		45.	B 103	000

			Left Hand	Right Hand
B		46.	B 100	000
		47.	B 11p20	400
		48.	B 103	456 (D#)
C		49.	B 100	400
		50.	023	450
		51.	B 020	400
		52.	B 103	406
C#		53.	023	400 C
		54.	B 000	400
		55.	½23	400
		56.	B 003x	000
		57.	½23	406 C#
D		58.	½23	000 (C)
		59.	023	000 (C)
		60.	B 100	45x0
		61.	B 12x0	400
D#		62.	½23 B	056
		63.	½23 G#	000 C
		64.	½23	4x00 (C)
E		65.	A ½23 G# D#	056
		66.	A ½23 (B) ½20	4x56 D# / 000
F		67.	A ½20 G# D#	056
		68.	A ½20 (B)	4x56 D#
		69.	A ½20 G#	056 D#
F#		70.	A 120	456x (C)
		71.	A ½20	400 C
		72.	A 120	406
G		73.	A 103	400
		74.	A 11p00 (G#)	400 C
		75.	A ½00 G# D#	400 C
G#		76.	A 103 B	056
		77.	A 100	400 (C)
		78.	A 103	006 C
A		79.	A 003 (B)	056 (D#)
		80.	A 000	400
		81.	A ½03 G#	006 D#
		82.	A ½03 B	4x06

CLARINET FINGERING CHART

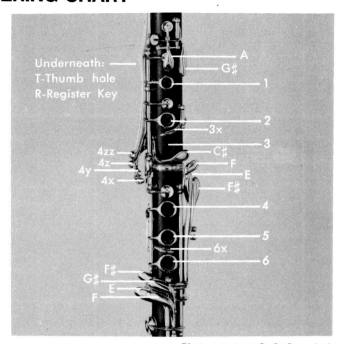

Underneath: ———
T—Thumb hole
R—Register Key

x,y,z—indicate keys operated by one of the fingers normally covering a hole. When they are used the hole is left open.

A, G-sharp operated by 1st finger; T—thumb hole, and R—Register key by left thumb; E, F, F-sharp, and G-sharp by little fingers.

Fingerings are numbered and referred to in the text under notes to indicate special usage.

Photo courtesy C. G. Conn Ltd.

			Left Hand	Right Hand
E		1.	T 123 E	456
		2.	T 123	456 E
F		3.	T 123	456 F
		4.	T 123 F	456
F#		5.	T 123 F#	456
		6.	T 123	456 F#
G		7.	T 123	456
G#		8.	T 123	456 G#
A		9.	T 123	450
A#		10.	T 123	400

			Left Hand	Right Hand
B		11.	T 123	050
		12.	T 123	406x
C		13.	T 123	000
C#		14.	T 123 C#	000
D		15.	T 120	000
D#		16.	T 120	4x00
		17.	T 123x	000
		18.	T 100	400
E		19.	T 100	000
F		20.	T 000	000

			Left Hand	Right Hand
F#		21.	100	000
		22.	T 000	4xy00
G		23.	000	000
G#		24.	G#00	000
A		25.	A 00	000
A#		26.	RA 00	000
		27.	A 00	4z00
B		28.	TR 123 E	456
		29.	TR 123	456 E
C		30.	TR 123	456 F
		31.	TR 123 F	456
C#		32.	TR 123 F	456
		33.	TR 123	456 F#
D		34.	TR 123	456
D#		35.	TR 123	456 G#
E		36.	TR 123	450
F		37.	TR 123	400
F#		38.	TR 123	050
		39.	TR 123	406x

			Left Hand	Right Hand
G		40.	TR 123	000
G#		41.	TR 123 C#	000
A		42.	TR 120	000
A#		43.	TR 120	4x00
		44.	TR 123x	000
		45.	TR 100	400
B		46.	TR 100	000
C		47.	TR 000	000
C#		48.	TR 023	450
		49.	TR 000	4xy00
D		50.	TR 023	400 G#
D#		51.	TR 023	406x G#
		52.	TR 023	006 G#
		53.	TR 023	050 G#
E		54.	TR 023	000 G#
F		55.	TR 023 C#	000 G#
		56.	TR 123 C#	456
F#		57.	TR 020	000 G#
		58.	TR 120	456 G#
G		59.	TR 020	450 G#
		60.	TR 100	450 G#
		61.	TR 100	400 G#

			Left Hand	Right Hand
G♯		62.	TR 023 F♯	406
		63.	TR 023	050 F
		64.	TR 023	406x G♯
		65.	TR 023	400 F♯
A		66.	TR 023	000 F
		67.	TR 023	000 F♯
		68.	TR 023	4x00 F♯
A♯		69.	TR G♯ 23 C♯	000 G♯ or F♯
		70.	TR 123 C♯	456 F or G♯
		71.	TR 123	456 F
B		72.	TR G♯ 120 (F♯)	450 (G♯)
		73.	TR G♯ 120 C♯	450 G♯
		74.	TR 020 F♯	450 G♯
C		75.	TR G♯ 100	400 F♯
		76.	TR G♯ 000	400 G♯
		77.	TR 103x	406x G♯
		78.	TR A 100	4(5)0 G♯

SAXOPHONE FINGERING CHART

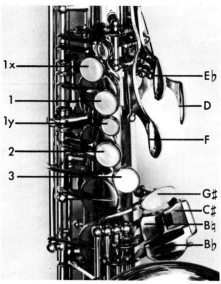

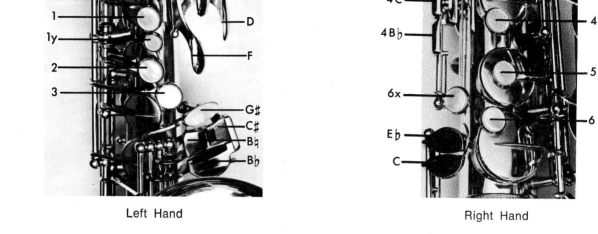

Left Hand

Right Hand

x, y—indicate keys operated by one of the fingers normally covering a hole. When they are used the hole is left open.

( )—Parenthesis indicate that use of that key is optional in that fingering, depending on intonation and resonance on a particular instrument.

			Left Hand	Right Hand
B♭		1.	123 B♭	456 C
B		2.	123 B	456 C
C		3.	123	456 C
C♯		4.	123 C♯	456 C
D		5.	123	456
D♯		6.	123	456 E♭
E		7.	123	450

			Left Hand	Right Hand
F		8.	123	400
F♯		9. 10.	123 123	050 406x
G		11.	123	000
G♯		12.	123 G♯	000
A		13.	120	000
A♯		14. 15. 16. 17.	120 100 100 11y00	4B♭ 00 400 050 000
B		18.	100	000

198

			Left Hand	Right Hand
C		19.	020	000
		20.	100	4C00
		21.	T 123	456 C
C#		22.	000	000
		23.	T 123 C#	456 C
D		24.	T 123	456
D#		25.	T 123	456 E♭
E		26.	T 123	450
F		27.	T 123	400
F#		28.	T 123	050
		29.	T 123	406x
G		30.	T 123	000
G#		31.	T 123 G#	000

			Left Hand	Right Hand
A		32.	T 120	000
A#		33.	T 120	4B♭ 00
		34.	T 100	400
		35.	T 100	050
		36.	T 11y00	000
B		37.	T 100	000
C		38.	T 020	000
		39.	T 100	4C00
C#		40.	T 000	000
D		41.	T D000	000
D#		42.	T DE♭ 000	000
E		43.	T DE♭ 000	4E 000
		44.	T 1x23	000
		45.	T F 000	000
		46.	T D 1x00	000
F		47.	T DE♭F 000	4E 000
		48.	T 1x20	000

BASSOON FINGERING CHART

Left Thumb

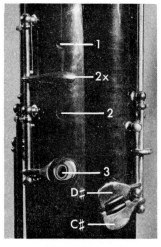

Left Hand

Right Thumb

Right Hand

x—indicates key operated by one of the fingers normally covering a hole. When they are used the hole is left open.

(   )—Parenthesis indicate that use of that key is optional

in that fingering, depending on intonation and resonance on a particular instrument.

Fingerings are numbered and referred to in the text under notes to indicate special usage.

			Left Thumb	Left Fingers	Right Thumb	Right Fingers
Bb	𝄢 ♭𝅗𝅥	1.	B Bb	123	E	456 F
B	𝅗𝅥	2.	B	123	E	456 F
C	𝅝	3.	C	123	E	456 F

			Left Thumb	Left Fingers	Right Thumb	Right Fingers
C♯	♯𝅗𝅥 ♭𝅗𝅥	4.	C	123 C♯	E	456 F
D	𝅗𝅥	5.	D	123	E	456 F
D♯	♯𝅗𝅥 ♭𝅗𝅥	6.	D	123 D♯	E	456 F

200

			Left Thumb	Left Fingers	Right Thumb	Right Fingers
E	(staff) 7.			123	E	456 F
F	(staff) 8.		W	123		456 F
F#	(staff) 9. 10.		W W	123 123	F#	456 456 F#
G	(staff) 11.		W	123		456
G#	(staff) 12. 13.		W W	123 123	 G#	456 G# 456
A	(staff) 14.		W	123		450
A#	(staff) 15. 16.		W W	123 123	A#	450 456x
B	(staff) 17.		W	123		400
C	(staff) 18.		W	123		000
C#	(staff) 19. 20.		(Dc#) W (W)	123 123	E	000 4x00 F
D	(staff) 21.		W	120		000
D#	(staff) 22. 23. 24. 25.		W Wc# W W	103 (D#) 120 103 103 C#	A#	000 000 0(5)0 000
E	(staff) 26.		W	100		000

			Left Thumb	Left Fingers	Right Thumb	Right Fingers
F	(staff) 27.		W	000		000
F#	(staff) 28. 29.		(W) (W)	½23 ½23	F#	456 456 F#
G	(staff) 30.		(W)	½23		456
G#	(staff) 31. 32.		(W) (W)	½23 ½23	G#	456 G# 456
A	(staff) 33.			123		450
A#	(staff) 34. 35.			123 123	A#	450 456x
B	(staff) 36.			123		400
C	(staff) 37.			123		000
C#	(staff) 38. 39. 40.		C# C# D 	123 123 123	 A#	056 F 000 050 F#
D	(staff) 41. 42.			120 120		000 056 F
D#	(staff) 43. 44. 45. 46.		 C# 	120 120 120 103 D#		(4)56 000 0(5)6 000
E	(staff) 47. 48.			103 D# 100 (D#)		(4)56 000
F	(staff) 49. 50. 51.			103 (D#) 023 (D#) 100		450 450 450

Bassoon

			Left Thumb	Left Fingers	Right Thumb	Right Fingers
F♯		52.	W	½23 (D♯)		400
		53.		103 (D♯)	A♯	450
		54.		02(3) D♯	A♯	450
G		55.	W	½23 (D♯)		400 F
		56.	W	½23 (D♯)		000 G♯
		57.	W	½23 D♯	A♯	400
G♯		58.	W	½23 (D♯)	A♯	006
		59.		½23 (D♯)	A♯	000 F
A		60.	a c♯	123 (D♮)		006
		61.	ac♯	123 (D♯)		000 F

			Left Thumb	Left Fingers	Right Thumb	Right Fingers
A♯		62.	a c♯	123 (D♯)		450 F
		63.	Wc♯	123 D♯		050 F
B		64.	b	120 (D♯)	A♯	450 F
C		65.	b	100 (D♯)	A♯	450 F

202

Index of Musical Compositions